The Tilley Treasure

A True Story of Civil War Action in Missouri

J.B. King

RED ENGINE PRESS

Copyright © 2017 J. B. King - Third Edition

All rights reserved. No part of this book may be reproduced or transmitted in any form or by any means, electronic or mechanical, including photocopying, or within any commercial information retrieval and storage system, without permission in writing from the author.

All book material and illustrations claimed, exclusive of the material excerpts from the U.S. Government publication *The War of the Rebellion, Official Records*.

Library of Congress Control Number: 2017936406

First Edition Copyright © 1984 J.B. King
Second Edition 2016 - College Press, Missouri

Paperback ISBN: 978-1-943267-36-1
ebook ISBN: 978-1-943267-37-8

Illustrations by Susette McCouch

Photographs are property of author or used by permission.

Printed in the United States.

Red Engine Press

Dedication

The Tilley Treasure is dedicated to a pair of great men. The first is my father, James B. King, Sr., a proud American with a high value system. I am honored to be known as his son. The second man is a writer, photographer, and my former journalism professor at The School of the Ozarks, Townsend Godsey. Hopefully, he will give this book a passing grade.

J. B. King

TABLE OF CONTENTS

Author 's Foreword		vii
1	The Coins	1
2	The First Year of War	9
3	The Second Year of War	33
4	The Occupation of Waynesville	41
5	Skirmish at the California House	49
6	The Autumn of 1862	63
7	Confederate Raid in Missouri	75
8	Skirmish at King's Farm	87
9	Wartime in Pulaski County	93
10	More Pulaski County Action	117
11	Death of Wilson M. Tilley	125
12	Trial of Wilson Leroy Tilley	131
13	Miss Emily Weaver	185
14	Aftermath	193
Bibliography		217
Index		221
Meet the Author		249

Forward

Research for *The Tilley Treasure* began in 1973 when I first heard the story. As the years passed, I came to realize that much of the information about the treasure had become lost with time. I found the treasure and the Civil War went together, hand-in-hand. I found there were large gaps in the recorded history of the Union Army. The Confederate side was much worse.

In some respects, the local legends about the history of Pulaski County were of no help. I found too many cases where the recorded information was scarce, inaccurate, and often in complete disagreement. In several cases, I found major events which occurred in Pulaski County were completely unknown to local people. The only records existed on a state or national level.

I found myself with a file cabinet full of material and no real idea of how to use it. The evening of June 10, 1983, I attended a meeting of the Pulaski County Historical Society and found an answer. The speaker that night was Mr. Bob Priddy, author of *Across Our Wide Missouri*. Mr. Priddy spoke about the loss of Missouri history with the passage of each day. He challenged the Society members to record Missouri history before it disappeared. I decided to accept his challenge. This book is the result.

The Tilley Treasure is not intended to be a complete history of the Civil War in Missouri, nor of the Tilley family. While reading this book, I hope you will find the past history of Missouri suddenly seems much more real; more alive. I hope you can develop a better understanding of the Civil War era in Missouri. I hope this book will entertain you with the enjoyment of history.

Writing a book is not a one person job. I would like to thank the people who helped me with this book. Without their help and support, the book would not exist.

During the research stage, Marjorie "Dee" Lane, of the Kinderhook Library in Waynesville, managed to find every book for which I asked, no matter how rare. She found a key part in the history of the Tilley family and brought it to my attention. Linda Gifford of Dixon helped with the Civil War battles and with the material from her hometown of Batesville, Arkansas. Pat Peters, from the Missouri National Guard Archives, was a lifesaver in checking Civil War records.

Mr. Joseph Newkirk Morgan took time from his busy work schedule to answer my questions about the Tilley family. Mr. Michael Musick, from the National Archives in Washington, D.C., was very helpful in locating Union Army records.

My thanks to Judge Tracy L. Storie for his proofreading and historical comments. Warren and Betty Pritchett developed and printed the photographs I took for the book. Susette McCouch of Waynesville supplied the artwork and designed the cover.

My thanks to Larry Freels and Claretta Craven Crawford for proofreading and their help in understanding the process of creating a book. Barbara Gladwill had the difficult task of reading handwritten Civil War records and converting them to typed copy. The most difficult job of all went to Penny Nickle, who typed the entire book. She also had the full-time job of keeping the author's writing in line with the accepted rules of English grammar.

The credit must be shared, but the mistakes are all mine. If you have a comment or question about the book, please feel free to contact me. I hope you enjoy *The Tilley Treasure*.

James B. King, Jr.
P. O. Box 226
Waynesville, Missouri 65583

Chapter One

The Coins

Buried treasure! The words quicken the pulse and excite the imagination. Banish your thoughts of gold left behind by early Spanish explorers or of hidden loot from a Jesse James' train robbery. Our story concerns a Pulaski County, Missouri farmer who lived during the turbulent era of the American Civil War. The book records a true account of his family and the silver treasure he buried in a desperate attempt to retain possession.

Our story covers a troubled and violent period of time from 1861 to 1865 in the southern half of Missouri. It was a time when Union Army patrols from Camp Waynesville scouted from Houston, Missouri, to Jefferson City, Missouri in their efforts to find the enemy. During this era, gunshots were frequent and death a constant visitor to our part of the Ozarks.

Next to the birth of Fort Leonard Wood and the early years of World War II, the period from 1861 to 1865 probably ranks second as the most active and historic time in Pulaski County history. After reading this book, you may feel it ranks first.

Yet, it seems hard to understand that in 1861 Pulaski County, or more importantly, the city of Waynesville was just a dot on the map. It was an unknown place whose only reason to be remembered came from the fact the St. Louis to Springfield Road linked the town to the rest of the world.

With the arrival of the Civil War and the establishment of Camp Waynesville by Union Army troops, the city of Waynesville gained a measure of status, just as it would in later years with the arrival of Fort Leonard Wood. Yet ninety-seven years after the Civil War ended, the expansion of Ft. Wood led to the discovery of a hidden treasure. And so our story begins with an ending; the discovery of the Tilley treasure.

On Friday, November 30, 1962, earth-moving contractor J. W. Mace of Roby, Missouri was quite busy with his bulldozer. The construction of a new series of housing units on Ft. Wood in the officers' section of post, known locally as the Capehart homes, required good topsoil for new lawns. The Army decided to obtain part of this topsoil from a section of Mark Twain National Forest. This section of land was on the military post boundary line, four miles south of Waynesville on State Road Route H. The topsoil was located in a field which was part of the Roubidoux Creek flood plain.

While Mace scraped the topsoil into large piles, other members of the working crew loaded the dirt into dump trucks and hauled the soil to Ft. Wood. All work suddenly stopped when the work crew discovered that Mace's bulldozer had unearthed two wooden boxes. One of the boxes had broken open, and silver coins were scattered throughout the piles of dirt.

In an interview with a newspaper reporter from *The Pulaski County Democrat*, Mace said that two loads of dirt had been hauled to post. The dirt had been spread on the lawns before anyone realized what had happened. Between the discovery of coins on the lawns and those at the topsoil site, word quickly spread. Within a very short period of time, a large crowd of people and officials gathered in the field.

According to the Democrat, the larger box had broken open and contained an unknown number of half-dollars. The smaller box held quarters and half-dimes. The Democrat reported that fifty dollars had been found on post, while the field yielded another six or seven hundred dollars in cash. These were estimates only, since the large crowd had roamed the field as they pleased, and the total number of coins picked up was unknown. Mace said all of the coins he saw had United States mint dates between 1840 and 1861. The coins were in very good condition even though they had been buried for years.

As the crowd in the field searched for coins, a well-known local farmer, Joseph Newkirk Morgan, drove by the scene on his way

J. B. King

home. In a special series of interviews for this book, Mr. Morgan, who was 84 years old in 1984, talked about the history of the coins and the Civil War. Mr. Morgan represents a direct link to our past. As a youngster, he listened to the words of friends and relatives who lived during the Civil War. Now he gives us details of local history that cannot be found elsewhere.

MR. JOSEPH NEWKIRK MORGAN, THE GRANDSON OF MARY ANN (TILLEY) MORGAN. MR. MORGAN WAS BORN FEBRUARY 23, 1900, IN PULASKI COUNTY. HE HAS BEEN ACTIVE IN LOCAL AFFAIRS AND HAS BEEN A MEMBER OF THE WAYNESVILLE MASONIC LODGE SINCE 1922. HE CONTINUES TO WORK THE FARM ESTABLISHED BY HIS GREAT-GRANDFATHER REUBEN MORGAN IN 1828. PHOTOGRAPH BY AUTHOR.

Since the coins were discovered only two miles from Mr. Morgan's farm, he gave the field much more than a casual glance as he drove by that day of discovery.

In his own words:

Why, gosh! There was a big crowd of people out there, including two or three Missouri State Troopers. I know Trooper

G. R. "Dick" Knight was out there 'cause I talked to him about it later. I thought there had been a wreck or some kind of accident. It looked like a picnic out there. But my wife, Rose and I did not stop.

I knew the fellow who plowed up the money. I knew him real well; "Jap" Mace from Roby. Jap told me they were plowing up land to make lawns for the officers' homes on post. Jap said he didn't know he'd plowed up the money until he looked back and saw the sun shining on it. He said it looked like bottle caps laying in the sun. Jap said it was bright, shiny money, and really glistened.

Jap told me the big box was about four inches wide and eighteen inches long. He said the bulldozer blade had cut the top off the big box, and scattered the money. I never saw the boxes, but Dru Pippin of Waynesville got one of the boxes. And, Dru told me later they were made out of walnut. He said someone had used a drill bit to make a hole from the top of the box, and the box was held together by wooden pins. No nails were in the box.

Dru also told me that for years before the discovery of the coins, he and Roy Wilson of Waynesville had dug in the field trying to find the hidden money, but he guessed they just did not dig deep enough.

I don't know what happened to the second box, but I've always regretted not stopping that day 'cause, you see, the coins came from my family. My great grandpa, Wilson Tilley, buried the money during the Civil War. He never told his wife where the silver was hidden and, after he was killed, she could not find it. She did know where he had buried a little gold; between the gate posts into the garden. And she dug that up, but nobody ever found the silver.

The early records of Pulaski County are frequently in disagreement as to known facts. Names are spelled in several ways, dates of occurrences differ, and no two records seem to be alike.

After a careful study of the available written records, it appears that Wilson M. Tilley was born in Kentucky on June 27, 1807. His future wife, Elizabeth Tippett, was born in Tennessee on December 13, 1807. By the year 1827, both had moved to Missouri and they were united in marriage on April 12, 1827. They moved to Pulaski County in 1828 and settled on the bank of the Roubidoux Creek, about four miles south of Waynesville. Between 1833 and 1850, the Tilleys purchased two hundred acres of land in that area from the United States government.

The Census of 1850 records thirteen people as living in the Tilley home. This record lists Wilson M. Tilley as forty-four years old and from North Carolina. Elizabeth was listed as forty-four, and from Tennessee. The record shows eight Tilley children as having been born in Missouri. The children were: William J., age twenty; Isaac N., age eighteen; Nancy J., age sixteen; Chalotta L., age fourteen; Wilson L., age nine; Margaret E., age nine; Mahala L., age six; and Missaniah S., age one. The census record also shows three other children, thought to be cousins, living with Wilson Tilley. They were: William F. Vaughn, age eleven; Jasper Vaughn, age nine; and Vandiver T. Christison, age one.

In contrast, the Census of 1860 lists the entire household as: Wilson L. Tilley, fifty-two; Elizabeth, fifty-two; Chalotta, twenty-one; Mahala, seventeen; Missaniah, eleven; and Jasper Vaughn, sixteen.

A comparison of the 1850 and 1860 census records show that during the ten year span Wilson and Elizabeth Tilley both gained eight years of age. Chalotta gained seven years, Mahala gained eleven years, and Missaniah aged ten years. The records show a drop from thirteen people in 1850, to only six people living in the Tilley home in 1860.

While farming and raising a large family, Wilson M. Tilley was also concerned with the spiritual needs of his community. In 1833, Tilley decided a church was needed and set out on horseback to locate a minister for the proposed church. His search ended in Bolivar, Missouri, when he found a preacher he felt was capable of the job.

The first meetings of the new church were held at the Tilley home with approximately twelve families in regular attendance. The church

The Tilley Treasure

A SMALL PART OF THE TILLEY TREASURE. THESE COINS WERE FOUND BY MR. MAURICE VAUGHAN OF WAYNESVILLE, MISSOURI, THE DAY THE TREASURE WAS DISCOVERED. THESE COINS ARE ALL SILVER HALF DOLLARS. THE ISSUE DATES ON THE COINS RUN FROM 1844 TO 1862. MY THANKS TO MR. VAUGHAN FOR PERMISSION TO PHOTOGRAPH THESE COINS. PHOTOGRAPH BY AUTHOR.

ONE OF THE OLDEST COINS FROM THE TREASURE, AN 1844 SILVER HALF DOLLAR. THE UNITED STATES MINT ISSUED ALMOST TWO MILLION OF THESE COINS IN 1844. ALL OF THE COINS PICTURED ARE FROM THE COLLECTION OF MAURICE VAUGHAN, WAYNESVILLE, MISSOURI. PHOTOGRAPH BY AUTHOR.

An 1862 silver dollar. One of the few coins from 1862 found in the collection. No coins with a later date have been found. Did Wilson M. Tilley bury the coins in 1862? Photograph by Author.

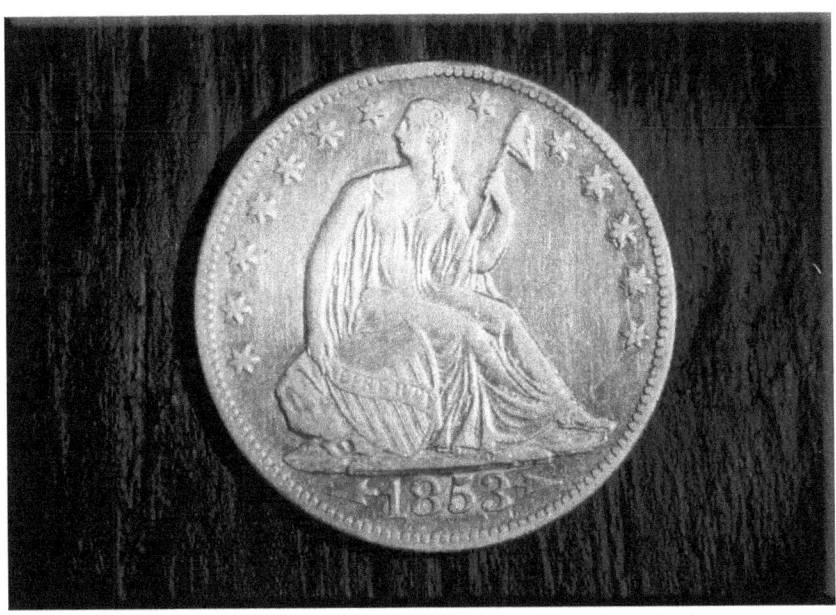

The 1853 silver half dollar has an arrow on each side of the date. The 1853 issue is the only one marked that way. Photograph by Author.

The Tilley Treasure

prospered over the years and still exists today. Despite the fact he was a devout Presbyterian, Wilson Tilley helped to found the First Methodist Church in Waynesville.

ANOTHER VIEW OF THE 1853 SILVER HALF DOLLAR. THE PRESENCE OF THE RAYS AROUND THE EAGLE ARE A UNIQUE FEATURE OF THIS COIN. APPROXIMATELY THREE AND A HALF MILLION WERE MADE. PHOTOGRAPH BY AUTHOR.

Chapter Two

The First Year of War

In order to fully understand the Tilley treasure, a degree of information from the national level and the history of Missouri becomes necessary. Proclamations and events set in motion by people in government or military command played a drastic role in shaping the history of Pulaski County.

The main factors which caused the American Civil War took many years to develop. The trail of events which led to the actual shooting started with the political thoughts of that era.

The Presidential elections of 1860 featured four major candidates and four major political parties. The issues were monumental; free slavery against abolition of slavery, and federal government control versus state government. The debates and political speeches were frequently marked by bitter exchanges between candidates. The country was divided into sections and each group felt they had the answer to the problem.

On Tuesday, November 6, 1860, the people of the United States elected Abraham Lincoln as the sixteenth President. The following day in Charleston, South Carolina, a palmetto flag was raised in defiance of his election. The course of the country was now set on a collision path.

In Missouri, the fall governor's race was decided by a narrow margin. Pro-Southern advocate, Claiborne Fox Jackson defeated independent candidate, Sample Orr, from Greene County. Jackson's pro-Southern sympathy greatly influenced his leadership at a time when Missouri was known as a border state.

The state of South Carolina passed an Ordinance of Secession from the Union on December 20, 1860. Members of Missouri's Twenty-First General Assembly met in Jefferson City on December 31, 1860, amid an atmosphere of intense political crisis.

The first act for Missouri government in 1861 was the inauguration of the fourteenth governor, Clairborne Fox Jackson, on January third. At eight o'clock the Speaker of the House of Representatives, John McAfee of Shelby County, convened the joint session of the Twenty-First Assembly to witness the inauguration.

The General Assembly moved to resolve the political position of Missouri by calling a special state convention to consider the secession issue. Passage of the bill on January 18, 1861, came as a result of a compromise. The original convention proposition had been amended to provide that any Ordinance of Secession would have to be approved by a vote of Missouri's citizens.

The following day, Saturday, January 19, 1861, the State of Georgia passed an Ordinance of Secession and joined Alabama, Florida, Mississippi, and South Carolina. The secession states had already served notice on January 8, 1861, that they would resort to armed force to back up their political views. This notice arrived about midnight on the eighth in the form of cannon shells fired at the United States Ship (USS) *Star of the West*, as it attempted to bring supplies to Fort Sumter.

From this day on, Ft. Sumter was under a siege. The Confederates in South Carolina felt the fort had to be eliminated since it gave the federal government a commanding position at Charleston Harbor. The federal government was equally determined to keep the fort.

In Missouri, the special state convention was the topic of the hour. The plan called for the election of three delegates from each of Missouri's thirty-three senatorial districts.

The election was held on February 18, 1861, the same day Jefferson Davis was inaugurated as the first President of the Confederate States of America.

The men elected to Missouri's special convention met on February 28th at the Cole County Courthouse in Jefferson City. The ninety-nine delegates felt the courthouse was inadequate for their needs. At the insistence of those delegates who favored the Union position, the convention was moved to larger quarters in St. Louis.

When the group convened in St. Louis, they were addressed by a commissioner from the Confederate government. Following a long and often bitter debate, the convention adopted several resolutions. One of these resolutions called for all Missourians to "labor for such an adjustment of existing trouble as will gain the peace, (sic) as well as the rights and equality of all the states." The convention delegates made a provision for a second meeting, if necessary, and adjourned March 22, 1861.

One of the stars to emerge from the convention was a prominent St. Louis attorney, Hamilton R. Gamble, whose strong pro-Union stand and speech impressed many who watched the convention.

Gamble wrote a major part of the report submitted by the session, and at one point he noted that federal troops should be withdrawn from "the forts within the borders of the seceding states where there is danger of collision between state and federal troops."

On the national level, the inauguration of Abraham Lincoln occurred on March 4, 1861. One of the first major problems given the new President was the plight of federal troops at Ft. Sumter. Supplies on hand were depleted and Union supply vessels could not sail past the Confederate gun positions. The time to make a decision was at hand.

In the following weeks, plans to send supplies to Ft. Sumter were made and canceled due to risk of war. In all of the secession states, property owned by the United States was seized by state officials. The list of property included ships, forts, customs houses, and even a branch office of the U.S. Mint.

On March 20, 1861, a highly troubled and greatly harassed President Lincoln found out he had one more problem with which to contend. His sons, Willie and Tad Lincoln, had the measles.

The national issue was decided on April 12, 1861, when Confederate guns began to shell Ft. Sumter. The Union troops replied with gunfire but were badly outnumbered in both equipment and manpower. After thirty-six hours of bombardment, Ft. Sumter surrendered on April 13th.

The commander of Ft. Sumter, Major Robert Anderson was quoted as having said:

Our Southern brethren have done grievously wrong, they have rebelled and attacked their father's house and their loyal brothers. They must be punished and brought back, but this necessity breaks my heart.

The news of Ft. Sumter's fall ended a lot of talk. People were now forced to declare their position and get off the fence. Like it or not, there was now a war to be fought.

Prior to the fall of Ft. Sumter, the same issues debated over the rest of the country were also discussed in Waynesville. Although the records are scarce, there do exist written records which show that about March, 1861, a large Confederate flag was run up on the pole opposite the Pulaski County Courthouse. Mass meetings were held at the courthouse and Dr. Lingo's drugstore. Theodore T. Taylor of Waynesville voiced with fiery eloquence his belief in state sovereignty. It appears that most county residents shared his belief.

In contrast, the Union sympathizers in the county remained silent since they were outnumbered. However, it appears that some men who were strongly pro-Union did leave Pulaski County and join the military units of other states.

In his inauguration speech, Governor Claiborne Fox Jackson had covered the political and military problems of the day. Besides advocating the special convention to determine Missouri's political position, he had also expressed concern over Missouri's weak military position by saying:

In view of the marauding forays which continue to harass our borders, as well as of the general unsettled condition of our political relations, a due regard to our honor and safety requires a thorough organization of our militia.

Thus, events leading up to the fall of Fort Sumter clearly show Pulaski County and the nation were ready to fight. The fall of Ft. Sumter was the final spark to ignite a nationwide war.

J. B. King

On April 14, 1861, federal troops marched out of Fort Sumter in the formal surrender ceremony. The same day a St. Louis area paper, *The Tri-Weekly Missouri Republican*, printed a statement which said:

> *No matter what may be the expenditure of life or money, the seceding states can never be conquered... a more unrighteous and unpopular war was never inaugurated.*

The following day, President Lincoln issued a proclamation calling for 75,000 state militia troops to enforce federal laws in the seceded states. His Secretary of War, Simon Cameron telegraphed a request for troops to the governors of all states still within the Union. The federal government requested that Missouri furnish four infantry regiments; a total of 3,123 officers and men.

On April 17, 1861, Missouri Governor C. F. Jackson sent a reply to the federal request which left no doubt as to his position.

Governor Jackson's message was:

> *Sir, your dispatch of the 15th instant, making a call on Missouri for four regiments of men for immediate service, has been received. There can be, I apprehend, no doubt but the men are intended to form part of the President's army to make war upon the people of the seceded states. Your requisition in my judgment, is illegal, unconstitutional and revolutionary in its object, inhuman and diabolical, and cannot be complied with. Not one man will the state of Missouri furnish to carry on such an unholy crusade.*

Also on April 17th, Jackson called for a special session of the Missouri General Assembly to commence May 2, 1861. The stated purpose of the session was to pass laws necessary to organize and equip a state militia and to appropriate the money necessary to put the state on a defensive war footing. Jackson also ordered the commanding officers of all state militia units to assemble their men on May 3, 1861, for six days of instruction and drill.

Jackson consulted with his militia commander in the St. Louis area, Brigadier General Daniel M. Frost. The two men decided they would seize the federal arsenal at St. Louis. The arsenal contained some sixty-thousand stand of arms, over two hundred barrels of gunpowder, and other materials of war. When Jackson issued his order for drill, Frost set up Camp Jackson near the arsenal.

UNION GENERAL FRANK P. BLAIR OF ST. LOUIS, MISSOURI. HIS ACTIONS AT THE START OF THE CIVIL WAR HELPED TO KEEP MISSOURI IN THE UNION. COURTESY OF THE LIBRARY OF CONGRESS.

Meanwhile, on the Union side men were at work to save the arsenal for the federal government. A major force on the Union side was Missouri's Free-Soil Congressman, Frank Blair, who was a close friend of President Lincoln. Blair determined the United States Army Commander over the St. Louis area was moving too slowly to save the arsenal. Blair contacted Lincoln and arranged for General William S. Harney to be temporarily recalled to Washington. The departure of

Harney brought into the top spot an unknown and relatively obscure officer, Captain Nathaniel Lyon.

Lyon was a very strong Union man and quite willing to work with Blair. Lyon arranged for more federal troops to be sent to St. Louis. They moved the entire contents of the arsenal to a place of safety in Illinois.

Next, Lyon and Blair decided to eliminate the threat to St. Louis posed by the seven hundred state militia troops at Camp Jackson. Lyon mustered approximately seven thousand troops and surrounded Camp Jackson on May 10, 1861. Lyon demanded Frost surrender his command, and Frost complied.

As the state guards were marched through St. Louis to the arsenal, a riot began. When the riot was over, close to thirty people had been killed and many more wounded. Among the crowd who watched the riot were three men the Civil War would make famous: Ulysses S. Grant, William T. Sherman, and Joseph O. Shelby.

Reaction to the military action against Camp Jackson was quick. Governor Jackson reported the news to the Missouri General Assembly, which immediately passed a new militia law. This bill provided for the enrollment of every able-bodied man under the Missouri flag for the defense of the state. A second provision of the bill authorized a loan of one million dollars from Missouri banks for the militia and the issue of a second million dollars in State Defense Bonds.

On May 13, 1861, Jackson issued a state-wide proclamation in which he denounced the action taken by Lyon in St. Louis. Jackson's proclamation was also a state-wide call to arms. In response to this call, two companies of state militia were formed in Waynesville. Pulaski County Sheriff H. W. Stuart was named as captain to head the first company. Prominent local attorney, V. B. Hill was named Captain of the second company.

Next, Jackson named Sterling Price to command the Missouri State Guard on May 18th. Price had been governor of Missouri from 1853 to 1857. He had also served his country during the Mexican War as a general officer. He was very well-known and a respected figure in Missouri.

As a reward for his quick action with Camp Jackson, CPT Lyon was promoted to the rank of General. He was authorized to enroll an additional ten thousand men to protect Union supporters in Missouri. In line with this order, on May 15th Lyon sent troops of the Fifth Missouri Infantry to Potosi. Missouri in Washington County to aid pro-Union citizens.

Meanwhile, Harney returned to St. Louis as the Commanding General. However, unknown to Harney, Blair was given an order signed by President Lincoln, which removed Harney from command. Blair was to serve this order whenever he felt Harney lost control of his area.

In an odd twist, Harney and the new commander of the pro-Southern state militia met in St. Louis on May 20th and 21st. The two men reached an agreement between them to keep order in the state. In brief, Harney would control St. Louis and Price would maintain order in the rest of Missouri. When Price returned to Jefferson City, he ordered the return of all state units to their home camps.

The Price-Harney Agreement was destined to fail since it did not please the extremists on either side. Men on both sides ignored the agreement and continued to plot. On May 30th, Blair gave Harney the written order of removal from President Lincoln. Lyon assumed command of Missouri.

In a last minute measure to stop the rush to war, a conference was set up between Lyon and Governor Jackson. On June 11, 1861, the top officials on both sides met at a hotel in St. Louis. After several hours of debate, nothing had been decided or agreed upon. Lyon ended the session with very strong words:

> *Rather than concede to the State of Missouri the right to demand that my government shall not enlist troops within her limits, or bring troops into the State whenever it pleases, or move its troops at its own will into, out of, or through the state; rather than concede to the State of Missouri for one single instant the right to dictate to my government in any matter however unimportant, I would see you and you and*

you and you and you and every man, woman, and child in the state, dead and buried. This means war.

Following the harsh statement by Lyon, Jackson and his party quickly left St. Louis and returned to Jefferson City, Missouri. En route to Jefferson City by train, the party stopped just long enough to burn the bridges over the Gasconade and Osage Rivers. When Jackson arrived in Jefferson City, he issued a call to arms for all Missouri citizens to resist the forthcoming federal invasion of Missouri. Jackson requested fifty-thousand more volunteers for the state militia.

Jackson made ready to abandon his capital. Jackson and Price had already decided they could not hold Jefferson City but would move all state offices to Boonville, Missouri. With new recruits and help from the Confederacy, they hoped to control the western half of Missouri.

On June 15, 1861, GEN Lyon, with two thousand men, captured a deserted Jefferson City, Missouri. Jackson and his state officials were gone, and their government would remain in exile for the rest of the war.

The following day, Lyon set out to follow the trail of Jackson. Lyon's troops met Jackson's state guard at Boonville on June 17, 1861. Governor Jackson ordered a charge by his men that Lyon's men defeated. Jackson's troops were forced to retreat to the southwest corner of Missouri.

The Battle of Boonville was a very minor fight, but the presence of several correspondents from large eastern newspapers made it a well-published battle. Overnight Lyon became a federal hero. While other parts of the country were gathering men and supplies, Lyon's forces were engaged in some of the first fights of the Civil War.

At the same time he left St. Louis for his advance on Jefferson City, Lyon sent a small force toward Rolla. The unit consisted of nine hundred German Home Guards, under Colonel Franz Sigel. Sigel's mission was to follow the tracks of the southwestern branch of the Pacific Railroad to Rolla, Missouri. The unit would then march along the Springfield Road in an effort to get behind Jackson's retreating troops. Sigel's force arrived in Springfield, Missouri, on June 23, 1861. No record exists as to what day they marched through Pulaski County.

From Springfield, the unit moved west. On July 5th, they engaged Jackson's men in a battle near Carthage. Sigel was forced to retreat. In that battle, the Union losses were put at thirteen killed and thirty-one wounded. The victorious Confederates reported forty to fifty men killed and one hundred-twenty wounded. The victory meant Governor Jackson's troops could not be trapped. Sigel's troops retreated to Springfield and waited for the arrival of Lyon.

UNION GENERAL FRANZ SIGEL COMMANDED SOME OF THE FIRST FEDERAL TROOPS TO MARCH THROUGH PULASKI COUNTY. GEN. SIGEL'S ACTIONS AT THE BATTLE OF WILSON'S CREEK, NEAR SPRINGFIELD, MISSOURI, HELPED THE CONFEDERATES WIN THE FIGHT. COURTESY OF THE LIBRARY OF CONGRESS.

Meanwhile, on July 1, 1861, President Lincoln appointed a new commander for the Department of the West, which included Missouri. The new commander was Major General John C. Frémont. Frémont was the son-in-law of a former Missouri Senator, Thomas Hart Benton. He was thoroughly acquainted with Missouri, since Missouri had served as a forward base for many of his path finding trips to the West. Frémont was also a good friend of Frank Blair.

During this time, the civil government of Missouri remained vacant. When Governor Jackson and his supporters fled Jefferson City, the government of Missouri collapsed. With the legally elected government in exile, a new civil government was desperately needed. Several methods of creating a new Missouri government were advanced and, after much argument, a solution was found.

When the special convention Jackson had called in January, 1861 had adjourned, a special committee had been set up to reconvene in case of an emergency. Members of this committee issued a proclamation on July 6, 1861 that such an emergency did exist. The convention was asked to assemble in Jefferson City on July 22, 1861.

Approximately eighty percent of the previously elected delegates met on that date and began the process of creating a new civil government.

After a political struggle between the Union loyalists and the few pro-Southern delegates that attended, a provisional government was elected for Missouri.

Missouri's new governor was Hamilton R. Gamble. The lieutenant governor was Willard P. Hall, and the new Missouri Secretary of State was Mordecai Oliver. The new governor was described as a conditional Unionist in his political views. Gamble felt Missouri should remain within the Union but should be able to exercise its own wishes and not be under the total control of the federal government.

In his inaugural address, Gamble asked for the cooperation of all Missouri citizens, regardless of past political views. He said, "It is utterly impossible that any one man can pacify the troubled waters of the state."

The inauguration of Gamble on July 31, 1861, provided Missouri with a new civil government.

During Sigel's march on the Carthage-Springfield area, Union troops had also occupied Rolla, Missouri. The city of Rolla was important to the Union because it was the end of the track for the Pacific Railroad. The railroad had reached Rolla in January of 1861. All supplies for troops in southwestern Missouri had to pass through Rolla. One of the Union soldiers at Camp Rolla was Charles Monroe Chase, a bandmaster with the Thirteenth Illinois Infantry. Chase kept a daily record of activities at Camp Rolla.

On July 26, 1861, Chase wrote:

> *Today has been a season of camps excitement. A few days since two of our companies were sent west to guard a [wagon] train of provisions going to Springfield for General Lyon's forces. We got word today that a large force of Secessionists at the Gasconade River fifteen miles distance had surrounded them and taken the train and companies. One of the prisoners brought in wounded yesterday was formerly sworn in as a Home Guard. His desertion may go hard with him. The Colonel says he may as well prepare to meet his God.*

Sunday, July 28, 1861:

> *Tonight three of the companies A, E, and I, who have been scouting in the vicinity of the Gasconade returned bringing thirteen prisoners and the contents of a store, with several horses and other property. One of the prisoners is six feet six inches high and looks warlike.*

The month of August, 1861 was a very critical time in the military history of Missouri. Union Commander John C. Frémont had ordered GEN Lyon at Springfield to fall back to the Rolla railhead if he felt he could not hold southwest Missouri. Frémont had cause for concern. A Confederate division, under General Ben McCulloch, had joined the Missouri State Guard. The combined force of approximately fourteen thousand men was advancing on Springfield, Missouri. GEN Lyon, with about seven thousand men, waited for them at Springfield.

While Lyon waited for the enemy, the question of supply became quite important. GEN Lyon's forces were short of food and ammunition. In an effort to reduce the pressure on Lyon, Major Alexis Mudd, Chief Quartermaster, First Brigade United States Volunteers, was ordered to take a wagon train of supplies from Rolla to Lyon's headquarters in Springfield.

MAJ Mudd was given his choice of two roads. The first road, referred to as the "high road," ran from Rolla to Springfield for a total distance of one hundred-twenty miles. The road was described as running over the ridge tops. The road had few ravines and no major river crossings, but good camping areas were scarce. The high road ran through barren country and was thought to be safe from enemy attack.

The second road was known as the "low road." It also ran directly from Rolla to Springfield. The road passed through Waynesville and Lebanon. It was described as a shorter route than the high road but was subject to bushwhacker attacks. The low road had more people on its route. It also had better camping places and several river crossings.

MAJ Mudd chose the high road, and delivered his wagon train of supplies to Lyon just prior to the Battle of Wilson's Creek. His wagon-loads of food, clothing, small rations, and shoes were well-received by Lyon's troops.

No record exists as to the exact date MAJ Mudd's wagon train passed through Pulaski County.

Meanwhile, the Confederate Army under McCulloch and Price camped at Wilson's Creek near Springfield. On the morning of August 10th, Lyon attacked the Confederate Army. The battle was described by one soldier as "a purty mean faught fite." The Union forces had two hundred fifty-eight men killed, eight hundred seventy-three wounded, and one hundred eighty-six men missing. The Confederate Army had two hundred seventy-nine men killed and nine hundred fifty-one more wounded. The Confederates named this the Battle of Oak Hill.

The Battle of Wilson's Creek turned in favor of the Rebel forces when GEN Lyon was killed while leading his troops. After Lyon's death, Major Samuel D. Sturgis ordered the federal troops to fall back to Springfield. The Confederate troops were worn out and did not chase the Federals.

At approximately 2 o'clock a.m. on August 11, 1861, the Union Army left Springfield in a retreat toward Rolla. The Union Army took with it three hundred-seventy wagons and over four thousand men. They reached Rolla on August 19th.

The defeat at Wilson's Creek and the death of GEN Lyon came as a severe setback to the Union cause in Missouri. A measure of GEN Lyon's fame was reflected in the Union Army's efforts to recover his body. On August 22, 1861, a small party with a four mule ambulance and a three hundred pound metallic coffin arrived in Springfield to retrieve the body. The party left Springfield on the 23rd. The coffin arrived in Rolla on August 25th and was then sent by railroad to the East Coast for burial.

The date Lyon's coffin passed through Pulaski County was not recorded.

On Friday, August 16, 1861, Charles M. Chase at Camp Rolla, recorded in his journal:

Men, women and children, with all their movable effects are beginning to pour into town from Springfield, having left well-stocked farms and everything save what they could conveniently bring with them. They flee before the approach of their enemy, leaving their property to supply their enemy's wants. Sigel has arrived within six miles and gone into camp with about six thousand men.

Following the big Battle of Wilson's Creek, southern Missouri experienced a period of relative quiet. Neither side was strong enough to advance. Both sides began to prepare for future fights.

In the month of August, 1861, William L. Bradford of Pulaski County and two of his brothers enlisted in the Missouri State Guard under General Price.

At the time of his enlistment, William Bradford had no way of knowing that one day he would become a son-in-law of Wilson M. Tilley.

J. B. King

As part of the planning for the future, the new provisional governor of Missouri, Hamilton Gamble issued an appeal on August 23, 1861, for 42,000 men to serve a six-month enlistment. Gamble's idea was for a Missouri State Militia to patrol the state and reduce the dependency on outsiders. Gamble had been angered over abuses committed by federal troops. He felt Missouri citizens should patrol Missouri.

Gamble's plan had two major problems. Since the Missouri treasury was empty, the federal government would have to equip and pay these troops. The second problem developed when the Union Army reviewed his proposal. The Missouri Commander, John C. Frémont, saw Gamble's action as an attempt to usurp his authority. Gamble failed to discuss his idea with Frémont prior to the public announcement.

Frémont responded on August 30th with a proclamation that soon produced a major controversy.

His proclamation read:

Circumstances, in my judgment, of sufficient urgency render it necessary that the commanding general of this department should assume the administrative powers of the State. Its disorganized condition, the helplessness of the civil authority, the total insecurity of life, and the devastation of property by bands of murderers and marauders, who infest nearly every county of the State, and avail themselves of the public misfortunes and the vicinity of a hostile force to gratify private and neighborhood vengeance, and who find an enemy wherever they find plunder, finally demand the severest measures to repress the daily increasing crimes and outrages which are driving off the inhabitants and ruining the State.

In this condition the public safety and the success of our arms require unity of purpose, without let or hindrance to the prompt administration of affairs. In order, therefore, to suppress disorder, to maintain as far as now practicable the public peace, and to give security and protection to the persons and property of loyal citizens, I do hereby extend and declare established martial law throughout the State of Missouri.

The lines of the army of occupation in this State are for the present declared to extend from Leavenworth, by way of the posts of Jefferson City, Rolla, and Ironton, to Cape Girardeau, on the Mississippi River.

All persons who shall be taken with arms in their hands within these lines shall be tried by court-martial, and if found guilty will be shot.

The property, real and personal, of all persons in the State of Missouri who shall take up arms against the United States, or who shall be directly proven to have taken an active part with their enemies in the field, is declared to be confiscated to the public use, and their slaves, if any they have, are hereby declared freemen. All persons who shall be proven to have destroyed, after the publication of this order, railroad tracks, bridges, or telegraphs shall suffer the extreme penalty of the law.

All persons engaged in treasonable correspondence, in giving or procuring aid to the enemies of the United States, in fomenting tumults, in disturbing the public tranquility by creating and circulating false reports or incendiary documents, are in their own interests warned that they are exposing themselves to sudden and severe punishment.

All persons who have been led away from their allegiance are required to return to their homes forthwith. Any such absence, without sufficient cause, will be held to be presumptive evidence against them.

The object of this declaration is to place in the hands of the military authorities the power to give instantaneous effect to existing laws, and to supply such deficiencies as the conditions of war demand. But this is not intended to suspend the ordinary tribunals of the country, where the law will be administered by the civil officers in the usual manner, and with their customary authority, while the same can be peaceably exercised.

> *The commanding general will labor vigilantly for the public welfare, and in his efforts for their safety hopes to obtain not only the acquiescence but the active support of the loyal people of the country.*
> *J. C. Frémont*
> *Major General, Commanding*

Frémont's proclamation of martial law ran against Governor Gamble's promise of amnesty to all who had taken up arms against the state. Gamble welcomed those who now wished to return in a peaceful manner to their homes and jobs. Since President Lincoln had quickly seconded Gamble's pledge, Frémont's proclamation angered everybody.

In a special dispatch on September 2, 1861, President Lincoln promptly revoked parts of Frémont's proclamation. Lincoln felt that the order to shoot those people found with arms was too harsh. Later he also canceled Frémont's emancipation policy.

On September 12, 1861, Missouri Confederate General Sterling Price began a nine-day siege of a Union garrison at Lexington, Missouri. During the siege, MG Frémont made no effective attempt to relieve or reinforce the troops at Lexington. When the thirty-six hundred federal troops at Lexington surrendered on September 20th, more people began to demand the recall of MG Frémont from command.

During September, the Confederate Army gained a new recruit when W. L. Tilley enlisted as a private in Company A, Pleasant's Battalion, Missouri Cavalry. The place of enlistment was Lebanon, Missouri.

With the fighting greatly reduced as fall approached, both sides turned their attention to money problems. Governor Jackson directed his homeless General Assembly to meet at Neosho and later at Cassville, Missouri, on October 21st.

The Rebel legislature passed an act on November 1, 1861, entitled, "An act to provide for the defense of the State." This act created ten million dollars in Defense Bonds. The bonds were to be issued in sums of not less than one dollar or more than five hundred dollars.

They would bear interest at a rate of ten percent, payable in three, five, or seven years. These defense bonds would be "legally receivable in payment of all taxes and debts due to the state."

A TWENTY DOLLAR MISSOURI CONFEDERATE BILL. THE SERIAL NUMBER IS 31, 317. THE ENGRAVED LEGEND IS CERES VOLANT IN THE CENTER AND LIBERTY AT LEFT. THE ISSUE OF THE BILL IS DATED JANUARY 1, 1862, AT JEFFERSON CITY, MISSOURI. HOWEVER, FEDERAL TROOPS UNDER GEN. LYON OCCUPIED THE MISSOURI CAPITAL IN JUNE OF 1861. PHOTO BY PRITCHETT STUDIO, WAYNESVILLE, MISSOURI.

A TEN DOLLAR BILL ISSUED BY THE CONFEDERATE STATE OF MISSOURI. THE BILL HAS BEEN SIGNED BY CONFEDERATE GOV. C. F. JACKSON. THE LEGEND IS CERES SEATED ON THE HORN OF PLENTY. PHOTO BY PRITCHETT STUDIO, WAYNESVILLE, MISSOURI.

While Jackson's followers were creating Missouri's Confederate money, the Confederate States of America appropriated one million dollars for payment to the Missouri troops fighting with Confederate forces.

A FIVE DOLLAR MISSOURI CONFEDERATE NOTE. THE BILL HAS SERIAL NUMBER 7004 AND HAS BEEN SIGNED BY GOV. C. F. JACKSON. THE LEGEND IS COMMERCE SEATED ON A BALE OF COTTON. PHOTO BY PRITCHETT STUDIO, WAYNESVILLE, MISSOURI.

The Confederates were not alone in their financial trouble. On October 10th, Governor Gamble reported to the provisional legislature that the state was almost bankrupt. Gamble told them that as of the end of September the treasury was down to only $21,422.73. The provisional legislature responded to Governor Gamble's plea, and they authorized the issue of one million dollars in warrants. These financial warrants were to be a short term measure and were to be destroyed when received by the state in payment of taxes. The legislature also authorized Governor Gamble to issue a second million in Union Defense Bonds of Missouri. These bonds were to be redeemed in ten years at seven percent interest.

Meanwhile, on November 2, 1861, MG John C. Frémont was camped at Springfield, Missouri. The forces of GEN Price were within sixty miles of Springfield and it appeared Frémont would at last fight the Confederates. However, this hope ended on November 2nd when a messenger from the war department in Washington, D.C. handed Frémont an order relieving him of command. The same order placed MG David Hunter in temporary command of the Department of the West.

As Frémont's ex-troops began a retreat from Springfield back to Rolla in November of 1861, they were accompanied by a correspondent from the *New York Herald*. As the reporter, Thomas W. Knox rode with the troops he "found many houses deserted, or tenanted only by women and children. Frequently the crops were standing, ungathered in the field. Fences were prostrated, and there was no effort to restore them." Knox also said, "The desolation of that region was just beginning."

The last three months of 1861 were marked by a number of small skirmishes in the counties located close to Pulaski County. One of the first fights reported occurred on October 13th at a place known as Dutch Hollow or Monday Hollow. The location given in the field reports filed by the officers involved in the fighting placed this fight as occurring twenty miles east of Lebanon, Missouri.

In that engagement, Union Major Clark Wright, Frémont's Battalion, Missouri Cavalry, attacked approximately five hundred Rebels. The Confederate loss was given as sixteen men killed and thirty more wounded. MAJ Wright also captured thirty-seven horses and thirty-two prisoners. Union loss was one man killed and one man wounded.

In another related battle on October 14th, Union forces surrounded the town of Linn Creek, Missouri. MAJ Wright demanded the surrender of the town and was immediately fired upon. In his report, Wright said the fight only lasted thirty minutes, but "the scene was a wild one." MAJ Wright reported no injury on either side, but did report he captured thirty-seven prisoners.

This fight led to another action near Linn Creek on October 15th. Several Union companies launched an attack upon a large Rebel group and scattered them. Confederate losses were thirty-nine killed, twenty-nine wounded, and fifty-one men taken prisoner. The Union loss was one man killed.

Again, on October 16th, another small skirmish was fought near Linn Creek. A small party of MAJ Wright's men was captured while gathering corn. One man escaped capture and brought the news back to MAJ Wright. A short time later, a fifteen-man patrol led by Lieutenant Kirby attacked the forty-five-man Rebel force. The Union prisoners were freed and five Rebels were killed.

MAJ Wright identified the dead men as:

John W. Candy from Buffalo, Dallas County, belongs to Jones' command; First Lieut. Fountain Maysfield, Dallas County; Carmelite Preacher Murline, Dallas County; three others unknown. Severely wounded George Miller, Dallas County, School Commissioner.

Union loss was one man, slightly wounded.

On November 1, 1861, Colonel G. M. Dodge, the commander of the Union Army camp at Rolla, sent four hundred-ninety men on an expedition into Dent County. The objective of the expedition was to drive Confederate Colonel Freeman and his troops out of Dent and Texas Counties.

COL Dodge placed Colonel Gruesel of the Thirty-sixth Illinois Infantry in charge of the force.

On November 4th, COL Dodge sent additional instructions to COL Greusel which read in part:

If the men who are away from home are in the Rebel Army or if their families cannot give a good account of themselves or their whereabouts, take their property, or that portion of it worth taking; also their slaves. Be sure they are aiding the enemy, and then take all they have got. They have aided and abetted Freeman in all ways, and most of them are now in the Rebel Army... Keep account of everything you take and who it is taken from... Be careful in taking contraband negroes that their owners are aiding the enemy.

During the evening of November 9th, part of COL Gruesel's infantry returned to Rolla. In his report, COL Dodge said they returned with "a large amount of property, stock, and several prominent Rebel prisoners. They drove Freeman from Texas County, and Captain Wood, in command of the cavalry, is still in pursuit of him." COL Dodge went on to say, "The expedition has proved a success, and I think has rid this section of a thieving, murdering Rebel force."

However, in early December, 1861, COL Dodge learned that Freeman and his troops were back in Salem. Dodge sent Major Bowen and one hundred-twenty men of the Thirteenth Illinois Infantry to Salem. These men did not locate Freeman, but did capture eight men who had been in the Rebel Army.

UNION GENERAL GRENVILLE M. DODGE. AT THE START OF THE WAR HE COMMANDED THE FOURTH IOWA INFANTRY AT ROLLA, MISSOURI. AFTER THE WAR, HE BECAME THE CHIEF ENGINEER FOR THE UNION PACIFIC RAILROAD. HIS EFFORTS IN MOVING THE AMERICAN RAILROAD SYSTEM WEST EARNED HIM THE INDIAN NAME "LEVEL EYE." COURTESY OF THE LIBRARY OF CONGRESS.

On December third, MAJ Bowen and his men were surprised by a dawn attack. COL Freeman and three hundred troops had managed to approach and slip through the guard line before anyone was aware of their presence. Once inside the guard line, they opened fire on the Federals. MAJ Bowen reported the battle lasted twenty minutes and ended when Company D mounted their horses and charged the Rebels. Freeman's forces fled, leaving behind six men killed and thirty wounded. The Thirteenth Illinois had three men killed and nine wounded.

On December 20th, President Jefferson Davis of The Confederate States of America wrote a letter to GEN Sterling Price of the Missouri State Guard.

In his letter Davis told Price:

The welfare of Missouri is as dear to me as that of other states of the Confederacy.

Chapter Three

The Second Year of War

On the national level, the start of 1862 was a time of dismal thoughts for both sides. Each side had hoped for a quick knockout punch to end the war. They now saw that the real work and real fighting had just started. Both sides realized they were in for an all out, no-holds-barred war.

The Missouri scene was pure chaos. Deposed Confederate Governor C. F. Jackson claimed authority to operate Missouri.

Jackson's Missouri State Guard, under GEN Sterling Price, patrolled a large portion of the state. The newly created Missouri Confederate money was in circulation throughout Missouri. All things considered, the new year looked good for the South.

The Union side of Missouri also looked good. Although his exact status was open to some legal question, Provisional Governor H. R. Gamble did have possession of the state capital. His legislature had also funded money for the war effort. As the new year began to take shape, Gamble waited for his newly created army of Missouri State Militia troops to take the field.

The Union side started 1862 with another advantage. Upon the removal of MG John C. Frémont from command of Union troops in November of 1861, a temporary commander had been appointed. That man, MG David Hunter kept the post a short time. The new commander of the Department of Missouri was Major General Henry Wager Halleck.

One of the first acts of the new year came when MG Halleck issued General Order No. 1 for the Department of Missouri. The order was released on January 1, 1862, and concerned the treatment of captured guerrillas and bushwhackers.

A part of Halleck's order said:

And again, while the code of war gives certain exemptions to a soldier regularly in the military service of an enemy, it is a well-established principle that insurgents, not militarily organized under the laws of the state, predatory partisans, and guerrilla bands are not entitled to such exemptions; such men are not legitimately in arms, and the military name and garb which they have assumed cannot give a military exemption to the crimes which they may commit. They are, in a legal sense, mere freebooters and bandits, and are liable to the same punishment which was imposed upon guerrillas by Napoleon in Spain and by Scott in Mexico.

The big news for Missouri as 1862 started was the beginning of a federal push to remove GEN Price's troops from Missouri. The new Union Commander chose Major General Samuel Ryan Curtis for the mission. MG Curtis set up a base camp at Rolla in January, 1862, and began gathering troops. The planned advance called for the Union Army to follow the Rolla to Springfield Road once again until contact was made with the Confederate troops around Springfield, Missouri.

In order to help safeguard the route of travel, the Union Army ordered the occupation of Lebanon, Missouri. On the morning of January 22nd, Lieutenant Colonel Clark Wright, Wright's Battalion, Missouri Cavalry arrived at Lebanon. Wright reported his forces took control of the town without serious difficulty but did report one Rebel captured. LTC Wright also reported a running gun battle in which Confederate Captain Tom Craig of Lebanon was killed.

LTC Wright relayed to Rolla some information of military value. Wright had determined that a four hundred man Confederate force, under command of a man named Rains had moved to Granby, Missouri, to operate the lead furnaces located there. Wright advised his headquarters that GEN Price did not have over ten thousand men in Missouri.

J. B. King

On January 26th, MG Curtis sent his twelve-thousand-man army west from Rolla. The push through Pulaski and Laclede Counties soon turned into a battle with Mother Nature. In MG Curtis' command was an obscure quartermaster officer who later became a famous Union General. Captain Philip H. Sheridan left behind a vivid description of the trip in his book entitled Personal Memoirs.

UNION GENERAL SAMUEL R. CURTIS, COMMANDER OF THE DEPARTMENT OF MISSOURI. GEN. CURTIS SET A STRICT POLICY FOR THE UNION ARMY IN MISSOURI WHEN DEALING WITH GUERRILLAS. GEN. CURTIS ORDERS WERE SIMPLE, "PURSUE, STRIKE, AND DESTROY THE REPTILES." COURTESY OF THE LIBRARY OF CONGRESS.

CPT Sheridan said:

> *The roads were deep with mud, and so badly cut up that the supply trains in moving labored under the most serious difficulties, and were greatly embarrassed by swollen streams. Under these circumstances many delays occurred, and when we arrived at Lebanon nearly all the supplies with which we had started had been consumed, and the work of feeding the troops off the country had to begin at that point. To get flour, wheat had to be taken from the stacks, threshed, and sent to the mills to be ground. Wheat being scarce in this region, corn as a substitute had to be converted into meal by the same laborious process. In addition, beef cattle had to be secured for the meat ration. By hard work we soon accumulated a sufficient quantity of flour and corn meal to justify the resumption of our march to Springfield.*

With the federal force once again moving toward Springfield, GEN Price felt he had to withdraw. The Union troops followed in pursuit and by February 17th they crossed over the border into Arkansas. The forces of Confederate General Earl VanDorn now joined those of GEN Price in an effort to stop the Union march. The result was the Battle of Pea Ridge, Arkansas.

The two sides had a combined force of approximately twenty-five thousand men. The edge in manpower was held by the South. The battle began on March 7th and ended the following day. The Confederates were forced to retreat.

In that battle, the Confederates had about six hundred men killed and wounded. An additional two hundred men were missing or captured. Confederate GEN Benjamin McCulloch was among the dead. The Union loss was two hundred-three killed, nine hundred-eighty wounded, and two hundred-one missing in action.

Union MG Curtis later wrote about this fight and described the end of the battle:

> *The enemy is again far away in the Boston Mountains. The scene is silent and sad. The vulture and the wolf now*

have the dominion and the dead friends and foes sleep in the same lonely graves.

The defeat of the South at Pea Ridge ended large-scale military combat in Missouri during 1862. Military actions for the rest of 1862 would be conducted by small units. An an example of the new trend, a patrol from the post at Lebanon, Missouri, made a scout through Laclede, Wright, and Douglas Counties. The unit scouted from March 4th through the 11th, 1862. The patrol consisted of forty-two men of Company E, Fourth Missouri Cavalry, under Captain Ludlow. During the eight-day trip the force engaged in two small skirmishes with Rebel forces. On the morning of March 7th, CPT Ludlow's men, who were camped at Fox Creek in Douglas County, were surprised by an attack. One Union man was killed and four others wounded. CPT Ludlow retreated to Hartville, Missouri, and joined with a patrol under Captain Heiden. Union scouts then came back to Hartville with information that the group who had attacked Ludlow was now in Mountain Grove, Missouri.

The Union force reached Mountain Grove about noon on the 9th of March, 1862. As the cavalry troops moved into the town, they were fired upon by men concealed in a tavern and the blacksmith shop. In the short fight that followed, the Union troops killed eleven Rebels and took twenty-one prisoners. In the loft of the tavern, the Union troops found some saddles and one overcoat they had lost in the surprise attack at Fox Creek.

One of the Rebel prisoners was Wright County Justice of the Peace, J.C. Campbell. The Union soldiers who searched him found a document in his pocket which read:

Headquarters Missouri State Guard
February 7, 1862
Authority is hereby given to J. C. Campbell to organize all of the men that he can recruit for that purpose into companies, to operate as a guerrilla force in the Sixth and Seventh Military Districts. He is instructed to disarm all Home Guards and other hostile organizations in these districts, and to place

the arms thus taken in the hands of his own forces. He will at the same time embarrass the enemy as much as possible by cutting off their reinforcements, scouting parties, and supplies. He is particularly instructed to prevent depredations upon private property, the unnecessary disturbance of any person whatever, either by the men under his command or by others, and he will report his actions to this army:

By order of Major General Price.

Signed by F. O. Gray

The Union troops found other papers of interest on Campbell. One set of records listed the horses, arms, and ammunition the Rebels had "pressed"(seized for military use) and sent to Arkansas. A third set of papers identified the Confederate Seventh Military District as comprised of eighteen counties in the southern part of Missouri. The Seventh District ran from Springfield to Rolla.

In a surprise move, on April 8, 1862, the commander of the Missouri State Guard, GEN Sterling Price, resigned. GEN Price departed the all-Missouri guard and accepted a commission in the regular Confederate Army. Price asked his men to transfer with him. However, many of the men did not want to join the Confederate Army. These men returned to their Missouri homes and, in numerous cases, they became bushwhackers.

In the early spring of 1862, Union Governor Gamble was quoted as saying, "Our state has been visited by a class of troops who come with feelings of hostility to our people and who under the guise of supporting the Union, perpetrated enormous outrages."

Gamble's remarks came as he continued work to establish his Missouri State Militia. On March 24, 1862, the Sixth Battalion, Missouri State Militia was organized at Boonville, Missouri. It was commanded by Lieutenant Colonel Joseph A. Eppstein. The unit was divided up and separate companies patrolled Lafayette, Cooper, Saline, Howard, and Moniteau Counties.

In March of 1862, the Union Army issued General Order No. 2 on the correct treatment of Rebel guerrillas. One section of the order read:

J. B. King

Every man who enlists in such an organization forfeits his life and becomes an outlaw. All persons are hereby warned that if they join any guerrilla band they will not if captured be treated as ordinary prisoners of war, but will be hung as robbers and murderers.

The Confederates were also involved in plans for future war in Missouri. On April 12, 1862, the Confederate States of America passed the Partisan Ranger Act into law. Under the terms of this act, General Thomas C. Hindman, the Confederate commander for the District of Arkansas, assigned a number of officers a special mission. These men were to slip into Missouri territory and act as recruiters for the Confederate Army. They were also asked to organize guerrilla bands to remain in Missouri.

On May 19th, the Sixth Battalion, Missouri State Militia stationed at Boonville was joined by several more companies of men. The unit was then reorganized as the Thirteeth Regiment of Cavalry, Missouri State Militia. The new commanding officer was Colonel Albert Sigel. The unit was then transferred to duty in the District of Rolla. Their assignment within the district included the town of Waynesville.

Meanwhile, in Pulaski County other events had occurred. On May 15th, James Carson was elected sheriff, and Hugh McCain was elected to a post as one of the administrative judges of Pulaski County. On May 20, ex-Confederate Missouri State Guard, W. L. Tilley, became a free man.

Tilley, like thousands of other returning Confederates, had been arrested by Union military authorities. In order to secure his freedom, Tilley had to take an oath and post a bond. The record of his bond reads as follows:

Know all Men by these Presents, That we W. L. Tilley of Waynesville in the County of Pulaski and State of Missouri, as principal, and of the County of in the same State, as securities, hereby acknowledge ourselves to be held and firmly bound unto the United States of America, in the sum of one thousand Dollars, for the payment of which, well and truly to be made, we hereby bind ourselves, and each of our heirs, executors, administrators and assigns.

Sealed with our seals, this twentieth day of May A.D. 1862.

The condition of the above obligation is such, that whereas the above bounden W. L. Tilley has been arrested upon the charge of having given aid and comfort to the enemies of the United States, and of other acts of disloyalty, and whereas the said W. L. Tilley has taken and subscribed the oath hereto annexed, and has agreed that he will not leave the county of Pulaski during the present rebellion, without written permission of the commanding officer of the nearest military post established by the United States authorities, and will report in person to such commander, whenever by him required in writing so to do; and has also agreed to give immediate information to said commander of any hostile movement, gathering or conspiracy which he may become apprised of; and to notify the officer aforesaid of any and all attempts which he may learn any person is making to enlist recruits for; or to induce others to join the so-called Confederate army, or give aid and comfort thereto. Now, if the said W. L. Tilley shall well and truly keep his said oath, and perform his other agreements herein before set out, then his obligation shall be void; otherwise of full force and effect.

And it is hereby understood and agreed, that in case the said W. L. Tilley should violate any of the conditions of this obligation, any officer in the military service of the United States, acting under the orders of the nearest post commander, may seize and sell, or otherwise dispose of any and all property of the above named obligors, to an amount sufficient to satisfy and discharge the amount above named, without having recourse to any proceeding at law.

W. L. Tilley (seal)

Chapter Four

The Occupation of Waynesville

On June 1, 1862, Companies A, B, C, and F of the Thirteenth Missouri State Militia (MSM), left Boonville on a march to their new post at Waynesville, Missouri. The unit chose a route of travel which took them through California and Tuscumbia. After a march of one hundred miles, they reached Waynesville on June 7, 1862.

The unit wasted no time in taking command of Waynesville.

According to local legend, they cut down a Rebel flag on the courthouse lawn and threw the pieces in the Roubidoux Creek. Then they rifled the stores and homes in town. Legend tells us the soldiers had first taken goods from a store owned by a pro-Union man named Hugh McCain. This store was located near the California House, seven miles west of town.

Local legend also tells us that the troops entered town from the east side. A group of citizens gathered on the western bluff overlooking town to watch the army. COL Sigel reportedly sent a troop of cavalry over to capture them.

The soldiers made camp and started to construct a fort. When completed, the fort was described as having an outer wall of earthworks. The inner walls were wooden timbers. In between was a water-filled ditch, four feet wide by four feet deep. The fort had a single narrow entrance which would allow only one man at a time to enter or exit. A hole was dug in the center of the fort that was roofed over with timbers and then covered with rocks and dirt. The ammunition supply was stored in that dugout.

While construction was underway, the top Union Commander in Missouri, MG Henry W. Halleck, departed for different battlegrounds. Halleck had created the new military District of Missouri on June 1, 1862. He left in command General John M. Schofield. Schofield immediately divided Missouri into five subdistrict's, each under command of a Missouri State Militia officer. Pulaski County was placed in the District of Rolla.

UNION GENERAL JOHN M. SCHOFIELD COMMANDED THE DEPARTMENT OF MISSOURI. HE WAS REMOVED FROM COMMAND BECAUSE OF A POLITICAL DISPUTE. COURTESY OF THE LIBRARY OF CONGRESS.

On July 6, 1862, LTC Joseph A. Eppstein and thirty men from Companies B and F, Thirteenth MSM, left the Waynesville post for a scout along the Big Piney River. Later that day they arrived at Wayman's Mill, located on Spring Creek twelve miles southeast of Waynesville. Eppstein then learned that a Rebel band under Coleman was twenty miles away on the Big Piney. Eppstein started after Coleman's band. While looking for him, he learned Coleman had taken possession of Houston, Missouri, on July 5th. Coleman was reported to have from one hundred to four hundred men.

Eppstein's report does not list a specific unit on Coleman, but the Rebel force was probably part of the Forty-sixth Arkansas Mounted Infantry, whose commanding officer was Colonel W. O. Coleman. His patrol area covered parts of northern Arkansas and southern Missouri.

Eppstein found no sign of the Rebels until he arrived at Johnson's Mill, thirty miles south of Waynesville on the Big Piney. His men took a prisoner who confessed he had just left Coleman's camp, which was nearby.

Eppstein and his men dismounted and managed to get within rock throwing distance of the enemy camp before they were discovered.

When Coleman's night guards fired on his men, Eppstein ordered a bayonet charge. The Rebels fled. Eppstein's men captured three Rebels and killed four more. During the charge the prisoner-guide, a man identified only by the name Bradford, tried to escape, "but was run through by a bayonet." The prisoners were identified as: William Hamilton, George Logan, and James Ormsby, all of Company A, Coleman's Battalion. One of the prisoners told Eppstein that COL Coleman had left Arkansas with six hundred men and had recruited about three hundred new men while in Missouri.

The Union troops were quite concerned about the presence of Coleman and his men. A major military necessity in the southern Missouri area during the Civil War was the safe transportation of supplies to the various Union Army posts. Coleman's presence was a direct threat to those supply routes.

As an example, on May 26, 1862, at Crow's Station near Licking, Missouri, a Union wagon train was attacked by one hundred-sev-

The Tilley Treasure

enty men under Coleman. The Union wagon escort was only eighty men. The attack started at 8 a.m. and, in a short time, nine wagons were burned and a number of men killed on both sides. The Union force managed to corral the train until relief troops from other Union units arrived.

A major problem was the huge area in which Coleman was free to travel. The Union forces did not have enough men to effectively patrol such a large area. More troops were requested. Companies G and H, Thirteenth MSM, were ordered to rejoin the regiment. The new troops left St. Louis on May 24, 1862, and traveled by rail to Rolla. They were retained there until July 13, 1862. On that date they marched to Waynesville.

The primary mission of the companies stationed at Waynesville was to scout for the enemy and escort wagon trains. Their assigned area of responsibility included the counties of Pulaski, Miller, Phelps, Texas, Wright, and Laclede. However, under pursuit conditions they could go almost anywhere.

Meanwhile, the Union troops continued to chase Coleman. On July 25th, a detachment of Union troops, the Third Missouri Cavalry who were stationed at Houston, Missouri, found Coleman. The battle began as a series of small skirmishes and ended when a section of artillery, commanded by Lieutenant William Waldschmidt of the Second Missouri Artillery, opened fire with their cannon. The fight occurred on the right hand branch of the Big Piney near Mountain Store, Missouri.

In the fight, the Union forces under Colonel John M. Glover, Third Missouri Cavalry, killed eight of Coleman's men. They wounded 20 more and captured 17 prisoners. The Union force had one horse killed.

However, in his written report, COL Glover presented a new problem to his superior officers.

Glover wrote:

I make special mention of the fact that four of the prisoners had the provost-marshal's certificates and claimed protection under them, at the same time throwing down their arms, so they were taken as prisoners without arms in their hands.

This is the kind of material which is by degrees destroying our brave troops. They take the oath, give bond, kill as many of us as they can, and when swift vengeance, retribution, and justice are about to overtake them they ask protection from their certificates.

On the morning of August 4, 1862, another detachment of the Third Missouri Cavalry left Salem on a scout to the vicinity of Sinking Creek. A few hours later they surprised a Rebel camp and killed five men. They captured twenty-five horses and two wagons. This scout continued until August 11th. The officer in charge of the scout, Captain Thomas G. Black, recorded an interesting summation in his report. CPT Black wrote:

We have done a work in this vicinity that will not need doing over again-turned up thunder generally. The Rebels are going in squads of two or three on by-roads to Coleman. From all I can learn they are concentrating at or near West Plains, in Howell County. Twenty men can chase all the Rebels that are in this county at this time. We will be off on another scout as soon as we can shoe our bare-foot horses. It will be perhaps two or three days.

In other events, on August 29th, a small skirmish occurred four miles east of Iberia, Missouri. A force of forty-two Union men under Captain Long, Company G, Enrolled Militia, attacked a Confederate company. The Southern force was thought to consist of one hundred twenty-five men under Colonel Robert R. Lawther. His unit was the Tenth Missouri Cavalry from Shelby's Brigade.

The Union force routed the larger Confederate force, which dispersed and fled. The Confederate loss was one man killed and three men who were wounded and taken prisoner. The Union force had one man, Lee Whittle, severely wounded in the groin. His wound was thought to be mortal.

The months of July and August, 1862, had also been busy ones for the top military and political figures in Missouri. In an announcement of major impact, Provisional Governor H. R. Gamble issued General Order No. 19 which said in part:

> *Every able-bodied man capable of bearing arms and subject to military duty is hereby ordered to repair without delay to the nearest military post and report for duty to the commanding officer. Every man will bring with him whatever arms he may have or can produce and a good horse if he has one.*

In an earlier action, GEN John Schofield, the Union Commander over Missouri, had ordered that all Rebels and Rebel sympathizers be held responsible for damages done by guerrilla bands. GEN Schofield's intent was to seize and sell Rebel property to pay the damage claims. If a Union soldier was killed, the Rebel sympathizers would forfeit five thousand dollars. The rate for a wounded Union soldier could vary from one to five thousand dollars.

The money collected by this assessment would be paid to the soldier's heirs or to the wounded man. Under this plan, money could also be paid to any Union property owner who suffered a financial loss through guerrilla action. GEN Schofield directed each of his district commanders to set up assessment boards in all counties under their command.

These actions on the state level left few choices for the Missouri male between the age of eighteen and forty-five. He could take an oath and enroll for militia duty, or he could declare himself a Southern sympathizer and end up on an assessment list. The man could join a guerrilla band and fight, or he could leave Missouri. There were no other options.

On the national level, President Lincoln issued a proclamation on September 24, 1862, which suspended the writ of habeas corpus and provided military trials for "all Rebels and insurgents, their aiders and abettors within the United States, and all persons discouraging volunteer enlistments, resisting militia drafts, or guilty of any disloyal practice, affording comfort to Rebels against the authority of the United States."

On the same date, the United States Secretary of War created the office of Provost Marshal General. President Lincoln appointed a new commander for the Department of Missouri to relieve GEN John M. Schofield. Lincoln's new choice was MG Samuel Ryan Curtis.

Chapter Five

Skirmish at the California House

The fighting returned to Pulaski County on August 29, 1862, when the post commander, COL Albert Sigel learned that a large body of Rebels was advancing northward through Texas County. The three hundred- man Rebel force was commanded by COL R.R. Lawther of the Tenth Missouri Cavalry attached to Shelby's Brigade.

COL Sigel determined the Confederate force would cross the Springfield Road between Waynesville and Lebanon. His immediate concern was to protect a Union supply train of sixty-five wagons which was camped at the point where the Springfield Road crossed the Gasconade River. The wagon train had a very small escort of thirty cavalry troopers under Captain Smith. COL Sigel dispatched his executive officer, LTC J. A. Eppstein, with most of the cavalry troops available to protect the train.

COL Sigel instructed Eppstein to leave a picket [guard post] at the California House, located seven miles west of Waynesville. Eppstein was also ordered to place other pickets at regular intervals along the Springfield Road. The pickets would serve two functions; first keep the line of communication along the road open, and second, to determine where the Rebel force crossed the road.

The skirmish began at midnight when the Rebel force crossed the road near the California House. The Union pickets fired on them. The Rebel force split into two groups and fled. One group, under Captain Johnson returned to the south. The second group, under COL Lawther moved north. Sigel ordered Captain Richard Murphy, Company B, Thirteenth MSM, and his men, who were the last mounted troops at the Waynesville post, to proceed to the California House and begin the chase.

THE HOME OF EMERSON AND MARIE STORIE OF LAQUEY, MISSOURI. THE BUILDING STANDS ON THE SITE OF THE CALIFORNIA HOUSE. ALTHOUGH THIS IS NOT THE ORIGINAL CALIFORNIA HOUSE, IT IS BUILT ON THE SAME BASIC FLOOR PLAN AS THE BUILDING ERECTED IN 1857. PHOTOGRAPH BY AUTHOR.

In the first skirmish at the California House, the members of Company A, Pulaski County Enrolled Militia under CPT Long, killed seven of the Rebels and wounded several others. They also captured two prisoners at the California House. One of CPT Long's men was killed and three others were wounded.

CPT Murphy's troop followed the Rebel force north approximately eighteen miles until they met a Union militia force from Osage County. The Rebels were caught between the units and twenty-nine of them were taken prisoner. The chase continued north until a point some twenty-five miles south of Jefferson City, where the Rebel force scattered into very small groups.

CPT Murphy reported continuing on to the McKerk Landing on the Missouri River. Murphy felt the Rebel force intended to cross the river at that landing, so he had his men destroy all of the boats at the landing. He also sent nine more prisoners into Jefferson City under guard.

In his action report, COL Sigel announced the capture of the Rebel commander, COL R.R. Lawther. The Confederate officer had taken sick during the chase and had been left behind at a private home on the Gasconade River. Union scouts searched the home and he was captured.

COL Sigel's victory was complete. However, repercussions from the fight soon surfaced. Rumors of ill-treatment accorded to the Rebel prisoners reached all the way to Division Headquarters in St. Louis. The new Missouri commander, GEN J. M. Schofield, issued Special Order No. 120 to COL J. M. Glover, the commander of the Rolla District.

Schofield ordered Glover to demand a written explanation from Sigel. He ordered the appointment of an officer to investigate the rumored events.

COL Glover ordered COL Sigel to make a written report and assigned Major H. A. Gallup of the Third Missouri Cavalry, stationed at Rolla, to investigate. MAJ Gallup questioned the officers involved and submitted to headquarters in St. Louis a written statement from each officer.

The investigation began with a written explanation of the events by COL Sigel.

He wrote to COL Glover the following:

I most respectfully submit to you the following statement, which I already gave you verbally: Two weeks ago a band of 300 secessionists passed the Springfield road seven miles south of this post at night and were scattered by our pickets. At daybreak three prisoners were brought in by the pickets and a part of a company under command of regimental adjutant, Lieutenant Kerr, as also several guns, horses, etc. Two of these prisoners confessed that they belonged to the gang and that they came from Arkansas with the intention to go to North Missouri and join Poindexter. The third prisoner, a certain Williams, living on the Roubidoux, claimed to be a

Union man whom the rebels had dragged out of the bed and forced to follow them. I released him and ordered the others to be confined to the guard-house until sent to Rolla.

As the rebels had several times on previous days fired at our sentinels and the telegraph wire was cut on the same place where the rebels crossed I felt much chagrined that the pickets had brought in the two bushwhackers, and I reprimanded Lieutenant Kerr and the noncommissioned officer who commanded the pickets for not having obeyed my orders and yours, colonel, which were to annihilate the outlaws and to bring in no prisoners. Lieutenant Kerr who mistook these my expressions either for a hint or for an order to shoot the prisoners took the two prisoners out of the guard tent and shot them. It was my duty to report this fact, but as I ten days ago had made an application to headquarters for a short leave of absence on regimental business to go to Saint Louis I intended to report personally at headquarters in Rolla and give the necessary explanation at your office.

I disapproved of the course which Lieutenant Kerr took, it having been illegal; but as Lieutenant Kerr is a zealous and energetic officer and mistook the words I used I don't think him culpable. You are also aware, colonel, that prejudices prevailed against the State militia and that the public press accused them for having shown too much leniency toward the guerrillas. Certain parties did not even spare the general commanding with such accusations and the Chief Magistrate of this State saw fit to advocate a more energetic policy. I therefore do not regret that the two bushwhackers were killed, the same being notorious characters, but I acknowledge that it was not the proper manner to execute them.

In reporting on his investigation to COL Glover, MAJ Gallop wrote:

SIR: In pursuance of Special Orders, No. 120, from division headquarters, I have the honor to transmit the evidence elicited by an investigation made in accordance with said order, to wit: Statements of Lieutenants Thomas, Avey, Kerr, Brown and Reichert and of Captains Reavis and Walters. The investigation was made yesterday and I returned to these headquarters last night.'

I am, Colonel, your obedient servant,
H. A. Gallup,
Major, Third Missouri Cavalry.
P.S. Colonel Sigel was not present at the examination of the witnesses, although urged to appear.
H.A.G.

The first witness questioned by MAJ Gallup was Lieutenant Thomas Thomas, Company G, Thirteenth MSM. LT Thomas was asked to state fully what he knew of the taking and killing of prisoners at the post.

LT Thomas answered:

I was on the scout with Lieutenant Colonel Eppstein. The night I returned some two or three weeks ago Lieutenant Brown came to see me and said that the adjutant had detailed him by Colonel Sigel's order to shoot those prisoners taken on the scout. I told him that I should decline unless they were sentenced by some tribunal, a court-martial or military commission. At night I heard of a firing on the creek and thought our pickets were driven in, but presently heard that the prisoners were gone from the guard-house. I went to Colonel Sigel's tent to inform him of it and ascertain what was the matter and was informed by him that it was all right and ordered to my tent. The next day I visited the spot where the shooting occurred and saw the dead body of a man there.

Next to be questioned was Lieutenant Francis M. Avey, Company H, Thirteenth MSM.

His interview was:

Q: State what if anything you know of the killing of two prisoners, Blakely and Meadows, some time in August.

A: Two weeks ago last Friday, I was officer of the day. Adjutant Kerr came to me in the afternoon and told me that he wanted the two prisoners that night; that Colonel Sigel had told him that he, Kerr, had "to finish his job." After dark, I went to the adjutant's tent and took a cigar. While we were smoking Colonel Sigel came to the tent and told Adjutant Kerr that "it was time he was off finishing his job." The adjutant told me that he wanted the prisoners; that the colonel had ordered him to dispose of them and he requested me to go with him. I went to the guard-house with him and six or eight men and took the prisoners out on the old Rolla road. About one mile from town we stopped in the road and the adjutant went to get some water. We started for the water and after going a short distance came to a small cleared place in the path. Adjutant Kerr was leading the way. When we were nearly across the clearing Adjutant Kerr stepped back by the side of one of the prisoners, turned with his face toward him and fired with his revolver. At the same moment one of the men fired at the other and killed him. Several shots were fired after this, but it is not known whether any of them [took effect]. Only one of the bodies was found and I believe that the one Adjutant Kerr fired at escaped.

THE ILLEGAL EXECUTION OF THE CONFEDERATE PRISONERS IN WAYNESVILLE ANGERED MEN ON BOTH SIDES. HERE IS OUR IDEA OF WHAT THE EXECUTION SCENE LOOKED LIKE. DRAWING BY SUSETTE MCCOUCH

Q: Did you ever hear Colonel Sigel speak of the killing; and if so in terms of approbation or disapprobation?

A: Adjutant Kerr requested me that night not to say anything about it, "for," he said, "the colonel will give me hell if he finds out that I did not kill them both."

Gallup also questioned Lieutenant H. B. Brown, Company F, Thirteenth MSM, about the fate of Meadows and Blakely.

LT Brown said:

Our pickets were surprised at the California House. Colonel Eppstein had gone out to intercept a body of rebels that were to cross at the California House. The picket was cut off during the night from Colonel Eppstein and came in to this post. I started out with part of two companies on foot just at daybreak to proceed to the California House, six miles west of this post. Adjutant Kerr with one or two men went out before me. I met him two miles this side of that house. He had Meadows prisoner and I understood from him that he, Meadows, had come into some house there for breakfast and had been captured. Adjutant Kerr handed the prisoner over to me and I brought him in and delivered him to Captain J. B. Reavis, Provost-Marshal.

Q: Do you know what subsequently became of Meadows?

A: I suppose he was shot. Adjutant Kerr came to me a little while after dark and told me that I was detailed to take the two prisoners, Meadows and Blakely (who had subsequently been brought in by the pickets), out and to shoot them. I asked him by whose order, and he said Colonel Sigel's. I asked him for written orders and he said there were none; that Colonel Sigel had ordered him to make the detail and he had detailed me. I told him that I would see him at his tent, and asked the advice of Captain Reavis, Lieutenant Thomas and others. Lieutenant Thomas said he protested against killing prisoners. Captain Reavis said, according to his understanding of general orders, rebels in Missouri might be shot on the spot when found in arms, but if taken must be kept until tried by court-martial and could not legally be shot without sentence. I went to Adjutant Kerr's tent and there saw two or three men loading their revolvers. One was Corporal Tillett, of Company C, Thirteenth Missouri State Militia. I told the adjutant that I could not kill them and that I would not furnish the detail he required of my company for that purpose. I left his tent and returned to where I had left Captain Reavis and Lieutenant Thomas and told them that I was of the opinion that the men would not be shot, and then went to my tent and went to bed and to sleep. Some time in the night I was awakened by Captain Walters inquiring what that firing was. He said he had his company all out and expected the pickets were driven in. I told him that I had been detailed to kill two prisoners and that I had refused to comply with the orders, and that probably the prisoners had been taken out by another detail and shot. Captain Walters denounced the act in unmeasured terms and said that if prisoners were shot in such a way he would resign in the morning.

Q: Did you ever hear Colonel Sigel speak of the killing of the prisoners?

A: Not directly.

Q: Did you ever hear Adjutant Kerr speak of the matter?

A: I have. I asked him that same night if they were really shot. He replied that they were shot and buried.

Q: How long was this after the men were made prisoners?

A: It was either the night of the same or the next day, I cannot tell now which.

Lieutenant Francis Reichert, the Battalion Adjutant of the Thirteenth MSM, was also questioned by MAJ Gallup.

The interview was as follows:

Q: What if anything do you know of he killing of prisoners at or near this post in the month of August?

A: I heard several shots the night after I got back from scout (after) Lawther's band, and the next morning heard that two prisoners taken the day before were shot that night.

J. B. King

That is all I know about it. It was foolish business bringing them here, but after they were brought here they should not have been shot.

Q: Do you know anything of the shooting of other prisoners subsequent to the events you have just mentioned?

A: Yes. I killed two and wounded one when out in command of sixteen men. One of them was killed by my men last Monday and the other last Tuesday. One was Elijah Grossland. He lived in Heath's Hollow. The other men were James and Washington Lemons, brothers. One of them was killed and the other wounded, all living in Heath's Hollow. The circumstances were these: We found a camp of forty rebels under command of Captain Kerry. They all ran and we followed, trying to shoot the whole of them, but only succeeded in hitting a few, killing two, wounding one, and taking one prisoner. I took Grossland at Adams' house. I had been following Grossland ten miles. When I found him I inquired if he had any arms, and both he and Adams denied having any at all, but upon making a search a revolver with three shots in it was found on the person of Grossland and a musket under the roof of the house. I put him under guard, thinking I would hang or shoot him right there because I found him under arms and he denied being armed, but I afterwards thought I would use him for a guide. I kept him for a guide from about the middle of the day 'til about eleven p.m. of the same day. He had given me a list of about forty rebels in the vicinity, and when I wanted him to tell me where their camp was he refused to tell me and said that I must hunt it myself and that he would tell no Dutchman. My sergeant told him then that he would have to tell or be killed, and then he tried to get away in the bushes and one of my men shot him. This was on Monday. On Tuesday we found the Lemons boys, Washington and Jim. They both ran. One of them was wounded in the back and the other lay down behind a log and begged for quarter and I took him prisoner and sent him to camp with two privates.

Before they got to camp he tried to get away and they shot him. Grassland used to belong to Coleman's rebel regiment.

The Provost-Marshal of the Thirteenth MSM, Captain J. B. Reavis, was next.

The interview began with a question by Gallup:

Q: What do you know respecting the killing of prisoners by Colonel Sigel's orders? State fully and particularly.

A: Two prisoners were brought in and delivered to me some time in the latter part of August by Lieutenant Brown, of Company F, and I sent them to the guardhouse. They remained there till Saturday night. Saturday evening at about eight o'clock, Lieutenant Brown came over and asked, "What do you think about shooting those prisoners?" I replied, "Think hell; I don't think anything about it. It shall not be done." He replied that the adjutant had notified him that he, Lieutenant Brown, was detailed by the colonel's order to take them out and shoot them; that he did not think it was right and should refuse to do it. He then went to the colonel, and I understood the matter was settled against the shooting. The names of the men were John M. Meadows and G. B. Blakely. About ten o'clock, I heard several shots fired, but thought nothing of it 'til the next morning, when the bodies of Blakely and Meadows were found near town. I have since that time heard Adjutant Kerr say that he was present when the men were shot.

Q: Did you understand, when said prisoners were brought in, under what circumstances they were captured?

A: I understood that there was a gang of rebels crossing the road the evening before; that our pickets fired into them and scattered them. That morning Meadows came in to the pickets and gave himself up and Blakely was taken near the same place without any opposition.

Q: State explicitly the nature of the charges against those men.

A: They were charged with being soldiers of the so-called Confederate Army, to which charge they pleaded "guilty." No other charges were brought against them.

Q: How long were said prisoners kept in confinement before being shot?

A: From ten a.m. on Friday 'til ten p.m. on Saturday.

Q: At what time were you relieved of duty as Provost-Marshal?

A: On the Sunday morning after the prisoners were killed.

Q: Did you ever hear Colonel Sigel speak of the killing? If so, did he speak in terms of approbation or disapprobation?

A: In terms of disapprobation, stating that he did not approve the manner of the killing or the time.

Q: Did he ever make any arrests on account of disobedience of orders in that matter?

A: He did not.

The next officer to be interviewed by Gallup was Captain James D. Walters, Company G, Thirteenth MSM.

Q: State what if anything you know of the killing of prisoners by Colonel Sigel's orders.

A: About the twenty-ninth of August, I returned from Rolla and learned from one of my corporals, Corporal George, that a gang of rebels had passed up west of this post and that two of them were prisoners here, one of whom had given himself up to him and the other to the stage driver. I knew nothing further of the matter and thought nothing of it. At about nine p.m. soon after taps sounded, Mr. McDonald awoke me and said that the pickets had fired five shots. I got up and dressed and in the course of the next five minutes heard two more shots fired and at the same time heard my first sergeant call on the company to fall out. After this I heard two more shots. I saw no movement of any other companies and started to Colonel Sigel's tent. On the way I saw Lieutenant Brown and asked him what was the matter. After a little hesitation he told me that he expected that the prisoners were being shot. While I was talking with Lieutenant Brown, Lieutenant Thomas passed me on his way to Colonel Sigel's tent. He soon returned in high state of excitement stating that he had gone to Colonel Sigel's tent to ascertain if it was true that those prisoners were being shot and to protest against it and that Colonel Sigel had ordered him to his tent. I could hardly believe that the prisoners had been shot 'til I searched the ground the next morning. One of the men was found about a mile from camp north in a thicket, buried with his head uncovered and his feet sticking out from under the sticks and rubbish with which an attempt had been made to cover him. I have searched the ground thoroughly in various directions but have never been able to discover the remains of the other man.

Q: Did you ever hear Colonel Sigel speak of the killing of the men; and if so did he speak in terms of approbation of disapprobation?

A: I have never heard him mention it.

Q: Do you know of any charges against the prisoners other than that they belonged to the rebel army?

A: I do not.

Lieutenant William C. Kerr, Battalion Adjutant, Thirteenth MSM, was questioned by MAJ Gallup in the same fashion as the other officers. At the time of the prisoner killing, Kerr was described as 26 years old, 5' 10" tall, with light colored hair and gray eyes. Kerr had given his home town as Lexington, in Lafayette County. He listed on his record his place of birth as Toronto, Canada. He enlisted in the Union Army at Lexington on March 28, 1862. His interview was conducted on September 12, 1862.

The record reads as follows:

Q: Do you know anything of the killing of prisoners by Colonel Sigel's orders at or near this post during the month of August? State fully.

A: Two prisoners taken at the California House about the twenty-eighth of August were killed by his order.

J. B. King

Q: To whom was Colonel Sigel's order for the killing of those prisoners given?

A: It was given to me. One man to assist in the killing them was detailed directly by Colonel Sigel. I think his name was Tillett, of Company C. The others, I detailed by his order.

Q: How was his order given? Give his exact language.

A: I cannot give his exact words. He told me to take some men, and did not name any of them except the one from Company C, and shoot the two prisoners brought in in the morning.

Q: Who took the two prisoners?

A: I took one of them at the California House, or rather in the yard in front of the house. The other was taken by the scout that preceded me there.

Q: Who was in command of the party that did the shooting?

A: I was.

Q: How large a detail was made?

A: Five or six, under the officer of the day, Lieutenant Avey, Company H, who accompanied us.

Q: Were the prisoners both killed?

A: They were.

Q: Have you ever heard Colonel Sigel speak of the matter; and if so, in terms of approbation or disapprobation?

A: I have. He has told me that they ought to have been shot, but was sorry that they were shot at that time; that it should have been done in daylight.

A study of the records of COL R. R. Lawther's unit, the Tenth Missouri Cavalry, shows a listing for a G. B. Blakely. Blakely was a private in Company H, Eleventh Missouri Regiment Infantry Volunteers, who was attached to Lawther's command. He had enlisted on July 20, 1862. His Confederate Army record shows that on April 17, 1863, eight months after the prisoners were shot, he was at Little Rock, Arkansas. No record was found for Meadows.

While all of this was in progress, Lieutenant Francis Reichert of the Thirteenth MSM reported back to camp at Waynesville. LT Reichert and his men had been on a scout to the south of Waynesville and had clashed with members of Coleman's command. Reichert reported killing three Rebels and he returned with prisoners.

Reichert had also learned that the main body of COL Coleman's troops, some fifteen-hundred strong, were in Batesville, Arkansas, at the time. The Confederate force was engaged in active recruiting around Batesville.

Reichert felt COL Sigel needed to be made aware of a Rebel plot to invade Missouri with a large force.

Chapter Six

The Autumn of 1862

With the prisoner controversy concluded, the post returned to routine business. One major event that occurred near the end of 1862 was the completion of a telegraph line along the Springfield Road. The telegraph lines ran from Rolla through Waynesville to Lebanon. West of Lebanon, it passed through Marshfield, Springfield, and Cassville. From Cassville, it went south into Arkansas. The road soon became known as the "wire road."

Meanwhile, the tempo of war in Missouri increased in mid-September. Union GEN J.M. Schofield was worried about reports from his spies that Confederate GEN T. C. Hindman was ready to invade southwest Missouri with a force of thirty-thousand men. Schofield was concerned about a second group of Confederates who were moving from Batesville, Arkansas, toward Rolla, Missouri.

In a letter written on September 18, 1862, GEN Schofield discussed military tactics with General Frederick Steele, the Commander of the Union Army in Arkansas. Schofield wanted Steele to attack Little Rock, Arkansas. The attack would draw the Confederate troops back to Arkansas.

In closing, Schofield said:
With these suggestions I leave the matter in your hands. Please inform me as soon as possible what you will do. Unless something be done now I shall lose a large part of Missouri.

The commander of the Department of Missouri, MG S. R. Curtis, was also worried by this threat. On September 25, 1862, he sent Schofield a message.

MG Curtis said:

Dispatch received. You are so far from Helena immediate co-operation by Steele is impossible.

General Halleck must have supposed Steele was at or near his old point, Reeves Station. A move on Little Rock would be the best diversion by Steele. Give me reports of spies and refugees. I do not see how Hindman could raise so large a force and subsist it when I stripped the country.

Hindman is sharp in deceit and pretenses, his army was in wretched condition at last accounts. Spies direct from his lines give me full, reliable reports up to the time of my leaving Arkansas. But be on the alert; the wants of the rebels make them desperate. Can you communicate with the forces in Kansas? I want to get dispatches through to Gen. Blunt, who I suppose is at Fort Scott. See that your force is not known to the enemy. Caution commissary officers not to report or speak of number of rations.

Telegraph in cipher [code], and keep me posted fully.

With a major invasion of Missouri under way by Confederate forces, the post at Waynesville looked to the south and waited for the enemy. However, they were looking the wrong way.

On October 17, 1862, COL J.M. Glover at Rolla Headquarters sent COL Albert Sigel a telegraph message warning him of the approach of Confederate troops. According to the message, some two hundred Rebels had crossed the Missouri River at Portland during the night of the 16th. These men were thought to be part of COL Porter's command. They had been on a raid into north Missouri and were now trying to get back to Arkansas.

COL Sigel sent CPT Richard Murphy west toward the California House with seventy-five men. Sigel kept one hundred more men at Waynesville. As before, his plan was to determine where the Rebel force crossed the Springfield Road and to pursue from that point.

On the morning of October 18th at 10:00 a.m., Sigel was informed that Murphy's men were in contact with the Rebels near the California House. Sigel's force started west and ran into the enemy force. In the short fight which followed, Sigel estimated his men killed twenty Rebels and wounded twenty more. His men captured three Rebels and liberated two Union men the Rebels had taken prisoner.

Reportedly, the Union force captured "a 'secesh' flag, 2 rollbooks, some horses and some shotguns and Austrian rifles."

COL Sigel also reported, "I ordered the secesh population of the neighborhood to bury the dead and to care for the wounded Rebels."

Among the civilians who helped bury the dead was Mr. G. W. Colley. The place of burial was nearby in the Colley Hollow Cemetery.

Another action was fought during the same period in Dent County. On September 13, 1862, eighty men of Companies C and M, Thirteenth MSM, charged a Rebel force under COL Freeman.

Although Freeman's force numbered three hundred men, they scattered in the face of the charge. The Union force had three men wounded. The Confederates had fifteen men killed.

THE COLLEY HOLLOW CEMETERY MAY BE ONE OF THE OLDEST GRAVEYARDS IN PULASKI COUNTY. IN THE CENTER OF THE PHOTOGRAPH AT THE FAR END OF THE CEMETERY, UNDER THE LARGE TREE, ARE THE GRAVES OF SEVERAL SLAVES. PHOTOGRAPH BY AUTHOR.

With the fall campaign out of the way, the troops could relax and commanders could check into the operations of the local civil government. In Pulaski County, the month of November, 1862 was important because the local Board of Assessment issued a report.

The Pulaski County Board of Assessment was appointed on October 7, 1862. COL J. M. Glover at Rolla, Missouri made the appointment in obedience to General Orders No. 3 from Division Headquarters. The board was composed of three men: Thomas Turpin, William Wilson, and Hugh McCain. Their report was issued on November 28, 1862.

The report consisted of two sections. The first was a list of Rebel depredations. The board listed the loss to good Union people through the actions of bushwhackers. The second section listed known Confederate sympathizers in Pulaski County.

As an example, on July 31st, William Goodman had a horse with saddle and bridle stolen. He also lost one Colt revolver. The claimed evaluation of $187.00 was allowed. A second claim was that of Hiram Johnson of Tavern Township. On November 2, 1862, he had one saddle and one blanket stolen. His claim of $7.00 was also allowed.

Others who lost property were: Daniel Bray, Daniel Richardson, Thomas H. Watson, William Kimmel, Joseph Lakeway, Calvin Knetser, William Hammock, James Hammock, and Thomas Lounan. A total of $987.75 in stolen property was reported to the Board of Assessment. The entire amount was granted. Each member of the board was given $3.00 a day in pay. The total bill was $999.75. Exactly how these people were paid for their loss was not revealed.

The second part of the report listed the known Rebel guerrilla and secession sympathizers in Pulaski County. The list started with: Isaac Teeple, Jacob Teeple, William Black, William Stuart, William Scaggs, P. Snelson, Samual Helams, J. S. Burnett, Acasden B. Warther, O. Ogletree, H. Mitchell, A. Acock, Bartle and son, J. Ray, D. Burnett Lemons, Dan Allen, F. Blair, R. Brown, Thos. Brown, H. Decker Gray, R. Watson, G. Gibbs, Rev. David, A. Roland, and E. Hibbs.

The list of Rebels also included: S. Harris, S. Carson, D. M. McNabb, A. Mitchell, B. Ray, C. Colby, Geo. Colby, S. Berry, J.

Alexander, Thos. Stark, J. Knapp, A. Lusby, Stone and son, J. Wilson and son, L. Hamilton, William Huff, W. Rydon, S. J. Woods, D. Merell, William Lowder, Geo. Logan, A. Logan, J. Bryant, A. McCartney, E. D. Bench, J. Bench, R. Adams and son, C. McEll, R. Box, J. Campbell, Geo. Cambell, and T. Woods.

Once the list of assessment was made public, the citizens of Pulaski County had much to talk about. But one citizen did more than talk. He complained to COL J. M. Glover at the Rolla Headquarters. The citizen was Wilson M. Tilley.

The complaint he made to COL Glover was not recorded. However, Glover made some reference to the Tilley complaint to LTC J. A. Eppstein, the second in command, at Waynesville. LTC Eppstein was not pleased and wrote an immediate reply to COL Glover.

Lieutenant Colonel Eppstein's first letter said:

Head Quarters, Waynesville
November 22nd 1862
Col. J. M. Glover
Sir,
Your communication of the 20th for Mr. Tilley is before me. I was much surprised as to contents and not less so the impudence of the man who carried it. The facts of the case are simply as follows. The Q. M. ordered some teams taken for use of the post. The reason he assigns for so doing is that many of the mules are worked down and unfit for service which I know to be the truth. The proper course for Mr. Tilley to have taken was to report to these Head Quarters. But sir he had a reason for the course he pursued. He was apprehensive that his claims would not be recognized because his Negroes were in the rebel employ in Batesville,

Arkansas. Which Negroes were really taken in here by his son. It is a fact notorious that notwithstanding the extensive connection of which Mr. Tilley is a member with a single exception every able-bodied man is in arms against us. Mr. Tilley has had extensive dealings at this post and was always properly paid, although he refuses to take demand notes from

Q. M. Peck assigning as a reason that he was apprehensive that they would not be current long thus tacitly admitting his disloyalty. And what are his claims to loyalty. He is the General Sponsor for rebels in the vicinity. He is in constant intercourse with rebels. He has never given us any information whatever. We have reason to believe that his house was an underground of those who ran away to avoid enrollment. Taking it all in all his impudence is only surpassed by his insolence. Nevertheless, your orders are permanent and to them I readily acquiesce. I am sir

Very Respectfully Yours,
Jos. A. Eppstein
Lt. Col. Comdg Post

A few days later, on December 6, 1862, LTC Eppstein, apparently still involved in this matter, wrote a second letter to his commanding officer.

He said:

Hd Qrs 13 MSM Cav.
Waynesville Dec. 6 1862
Col. John M. Glover
Comdg. Rolla District
Col.,

Your communication of Nov. 2, was duly received, after perusing the same I am sorry to find that my letter in reply to yours of the 20th was misunderstood. The facts as far as I can learn them in regard to the Tilley case are as follows.

Quarter Master Rotert complained to Division Q. M. Peck, that he was short of means of transportation, applying at the same time for an addition or an exchange of some un-serviceable mules for some which were serviceable: To which Division Quarter Master Peck replied: "That he was unable to get all the transportation he needed and that he was sometimes obliged to press" advising Quarter Master Rotert to do the same; with this information it is reasonable to suppose that our Quarter Master thought it useless to apply in a regular way for additional means of transportation, and availed himself of the only means of providing forage for this post, and for this purpose he took several teams from this neighborhood without regard to Politics, intending to give the owners vouchers (as he has done before) when he returned them. The necessity for this step, I am willing for you or any other Officer to decide. Half of the mules furnished this regiment from the start were unserviceable, and I do not know how they could pass inspection. We have complained about it before but to no avail.

To provide a post like this, in a barren and mountainous country, with all the necessaries, is not an easy task, with such incomplete means of transportation and the result of such an undertaking would have been the ruin of the other half of our stock from over task. We are losing horses daily from the want of forage and our command is complaining bitterly against the Quarter Master and the Government for not furnishing the same. Again, you seem to doubt my opinion about Mr. Tilley's true character. You ask for "indisputable proof." Well Sir: it was not my intention nor is it yet, to bring formal charges against the man, or else I would have gathered the evidence in a legal shape, but I can give you some facts on which I formed my opinion: Would the County Commissioners have put Mr. Tilley's name on the list of Rebel sympathizers for assessment to pay the damages committed by Rebel depredators in this county if they had not had evidence to that effect? I accidentally met with two of these Commissioners yesterday and inquired how it was that their names were on a document which recommended Mr. Tilley as a Good Loyal citizen, when both of them protested against having such use made of their names: They say that Tilley swindled them out of their signatures, by false pretenses, in saying that it was a certificate about his honesty and good character to which at that time they had no objections. The names of these Commissioners are Judge McCain and Turpin. They are *willing to make affidavits that Tilley is disloyal and a Rebel sympathizer, and that he was looked upon as such in the county, they also say that there was no doubt in their minds about Tilley's knowing and acquiescing in the removing of his Negroes and horses South. I have made inquiries about Mr. Tilley's application for assistance at this post, for recovery of his property, and find that he told you an untruth: He simply reported the disappearance of the Negroes and horses to the Provost Marshall stating that he had no idea as to their whereabouts. Capt. Thompson Co. B, Enrolled Mo. Militia of this Co. (who resides with Mr. Tilley) was present at the time and remarked to Lieut. Estas (of his company) and to Lieut. Muntzell Co. F, of this regiment, that he was satisfied that Mr. Tilley's son knew all about the matter. When the Militia was ordered to enroll-the Rebels took a general stampede and ran South about (20) of them from this neighborhood, met by pre-arrangement, at the house of Mr. Tilley, but the old gentleman, was so much opposed to the going of his son, that he had no time to inform us of that movement, although they remained at his house several hours, and the distance to our camp was but five miles. I suppose he was afraid of hurting his son's feelings by so doing. We are about six months at this post, and several important moves have been made by the Rebels during this time, but I have to get the first report from Mr. Tilley yet. So much for the loyalty and veracity of Mr. Tilley.*

In answer to your question about the "extensive dealings and prompt payment," I have to say that Mr. Tilley was one of the few in this neighborhood who had anything to spare, and necessity, not choice almost compelled our Quarter Master to purchase where it was to be had. You complain of "mismanagement and depredations committed by incompetent, injudicious and unprincipled federal Officers and Soldiers": This is severe language, but very appropriate in many instances as I am sorry to say. I make no pretentions as to my

J. B. King

qualifications as an Officer. I am willing to be judged by my acts as a Soldier or Citizen.

For the past (23) years I have lived in Mo. with the exception of a campaign of (18) months in Mexico as a member of the 3rd Mo. Mounted Rifles. I have been engaged in the mercantile business for the last (20) years and by this means became extensively known in St. Louis, Jeff. City, and Boonville, Mo. the latter place is my domicile since 1850, and after General Lyon and Blair drove Price off from that place, and were preparing to leave for Springfield, they thought it necessary to keep Boonville occupied and for that purpose consulted me about the organization of the Home Guards. I saw the danger if we were left unprotected, and consented to shut up my store, and come to the aid of my adopted country instead. I soon had organized a Battalion of Home Guards, furnished them with uniforms, blankets and other necessaries because the Gov't at that time was not able to provide for the Regular Army, less for the Home Guards. Six months I kept this Battalion in service and very important services it rendered; but when I came to the Pay-Master General with an order from Maj. Gen Frémont to pay my Battalion, I was told we must go into the Regular Volunteer Service if we wanted to be paid. I did not like to be forced into the service in such a manner and thinking our State had the first right to our services, I enlisted with about three-fourths of my old command into the State Service, and not a cent of pay has any of my men or myself received yet. I was in command at Boonville for about nine months, the most part of that time I acted in a double capacity: as a Commander of the post, and Provost Marshall, and not one complaint was made against any of my acts or decisions that I could hear of, to the contrary I received letters from my friends as well as from Rebel Sympathizers expressing a desire to have me in command again at that post. I am as much opposed to the abuse of Military authority as any man. I know how to appreciate a citizens rights because

I had mine trampled upon heretofore: far be it from me to have any citizen molested if it is in my power to prevent it. There is as you say a great many bad and unprincipled men in the Army who require all the vigilance of a good Officer to prevent them from carrying out their mischief, but with all this vigilance depredations will be committed sometimes. Whenever I can find out the perpetrators I punish them and make them pay the damages and in some instances when I could not find out the guilty parties I paid the damages o·ut of my pocket rather than see a citizen suffer who has a right to our protection.

After giving you a short history of Mr. Tilley and myself, it does not seem to me that you should think strange "at my surprise," at such men as Mr. Tilley lodging complaints against me. As this communication is getting lengthy, I must close, but if I have not explained myself fully I should be happy to hear from you at any time.

With these few remarks on the most important points of your correspondence, I beg leave to subscribe myself

Your most Obedient Servant,

Jos. A. Eppstein

Lt. Col. Comdg. 13 MSM Cav.

With the end of 1862 only three weeks away, the Confederate government of Missouri suffered a setback. Governor Claiborne Fox Jackson had been with his troops near Little Rock, Arkansas, for some time. In late November, he caught a bad cold, which later developed into pneumonia. Governor Jackson died on December 7, 1862.

On December 24, 1862, a group of ninety-six Confederate prisoners of war left Springfield under escort to a St. Louis military prison. The group traveled the St. Louis to Springfield Road. One of these prisoners was Herîry Martyn Cheavens, who later recorded the details of the trip.

Cheavens probably traveled through Waynesville, for he wrote:

We passed through some very poor land at one point. In one place we found block houses and fortifications. We gained

J. B. King

some six additional ones at one town, one died, one was left at Rolla. On the 30th, we arrived in Rolla...

Chapter Seven

Confederate Raid into Missouri

In late 1862, Union General Frederick Steele was closing on the Confederate capital at Little Rock, Arkansas. In a move designed to divert Union forces, Confederate General John S. Marmaduke developed a plan for a cavalry raid into Missouri. Marmaduke's forces started north on December 31, 1862.

Thus, New Year's Day, 1863, saw Union forces throughout southern Missouri ready to meet the Marmaduke raid. The raid took approximately one month to complete.

On January 7, 1863, the Confederate force captured Ozark, Missouri. On January 8th, the Union garrison at Springfield successfully def ended their post. However, the Confederates destroyed a lot of military supplies and tore down the telegraph lines around the town.

The Confederate advance turned east. On January 11th, they captured and burned the federal forts at Marshfield and Sand Springs. The Confederate plan was to capture Hartville, Missouri, next. In response to the Confederate raid, the Thirteenth Missouri State Militia was ordered out of the Waynesville post. They moved south toward Hartville. On January 12, 1863, the Confederates attacked Hartville.

The fight continued most of the day. The Confederates had severe losses among their officer corps. One of the dead officers was COL Porter, who had recently raided into Pulaski County. As dark fell on the 12th, GEN Marmaduke, knowing federal cavalry troops were approaching in force from several directions, gave the order to start south. The raid was over. On January 18th, the retreating southern units reached Batesville, Arkansas.

The Tilley Treasure

CONFEDERATE GENERAL JOHN SAPPINGTON MARMADUKE. ONE OF THE BEST FIELD COMMANDERS THE CONFEDERATE ARMY SENT INTO MISSOURI. GEN. MARMADUKE'S TROOPS RAIDED INTO MISSOURI ON A REGULAR BASIS. COURTESY OF THE LIBRARY OF CONGRESS.

On January 13, 1863, the Thirteenth MSM reached Hartville too late to fight. The unit was sent south in pursuit of Marmaduke. With their horses already tired from the march to Hartville, they were unable to catch Marmaduke. COL Sigel gave the order to retire and the Thirteenth MSM returned to Waynesville via Houston, Missouri. Their trip lasted eight days.

In February, 1863, the Thirteenth MSM had to make the same trip. An alarm was sent to all federal forces that GEN Marmaduke's men were about to attack Houston, Missouri. LTC J. A. Eppstein and four full companies of the Thirteenth rushed to Houston. Upon their arrival, they found no enemy within fifty miles of Houston. The scare was a false alarm. The battalion returned to Waynesville.

On February 2, 1863, General Order No. 5, concerning the Missouri State Militia, was announced. This order created a number of changes in MSM units over the state. In one transfer, a company of cavalry known as the Schofield Hussars, under Captain Napoleon Westerberg, was attached to the Thirteenth MSM.

The second change read:

The regiment heretofore designated as the Thirteenth Cavalry, Missouri State Militia, will hereafter be known as the 5th Regiment of Cavalry, Missouri State Militia." The Confederate lieutenant governor of Missouri, Thomas C. Reynolds, issued a proclamation on February 14, 1863. In his message, Reynolds announced the death of Claiborne Fox Jackson and his own assumption of power as the new governor of Missouri.

In other Confederate action, the former head of the Missouri State Guard, GEN Sterling Price was ordered transferred to the Trans-Mississippi Department. Although he was now a full General in the regular army of the Confederate States, GEN Price was about to get his old job back.

The national scene for March, 1863, saw President Lincoln sign a measure for a new military draft. The draft act imposed a liability on all male citizens between twenty and forty-five years of age. There were certain exceptions for convicted felons, the mentally unfit, and men who held specific government jobs.

One of the interesting provisions of this act was the fact that for $300.00 in cash a man could purchase his freedom from the draft.

Or, he could hire a substitute to serve his enlistment for him. In one sense, the draft act was a failure. Only six percent of the troops serving the Union during the entire war were drafted.

The Confederate Department of Trans-Mississippi got a new commander on March 7, 1863. The new general was E. Kirby Smith. His first objective was another raid into Missouri. The Missouri scene in April of 1863 was marked by a strong statement from Union MG S. R. Curtis. He was concerned over the actions of guerrillas throughout Missouri. On April 22, 1863, MG Curtis said guerrillas, "deserve no quarter, no kind of civilized warfare. Pursue, strike, and destroy the reptiles!"

CONFEDERATE GENERAL EDMUND KIRBY SMITH, THE COMMANDER OF THE CONFEDERATE DEPARTMENT OF TRANS-MISSISSIPPI, WHICH INCLUDED THE STATE OF MISSOURI. ALTHOUGH GEN. SMITH'S HEADQUARTERS WERE LOCATED IN SHREVEPORT, LOUISIANA, HE FREQUENTLY SENT REBEL TROOPS INTO MISSOURI. COURTESY OF THE LIBRARY OF CONGRESS.

The next action in the war for Missouri began on April 19, 1863. Confederate GEN John S. Marmaduke and his men left Batesville, Arkansas, headed toward Missouri. The Confederates hoped their advance toward Rolla, Missouri would deceive Union troops. The plan called for a strong feint toward Rolla, but the actual plan of attack was against the Union posts at Houston and Patterson, Missouri.

After these small forts fell, the southern advance would swing east and attack a major federal supply depot at Cape Girardeau. During this time frame, small scouting parties would roam throughout southern Missouri in search of Union supply trains, telegraph lines, and patrols.

At first, the plan worked. The Union garrison at Patterson was surprised. After a short fight, the Union troops burned their fort and retreated. The Confederates turned toward Cape Girardau. The next objective was the Union gardson at Bloomfield, Missouri.

As the Confederates neared Bloomfield, heavy rains began. The roads turned into deep mud. Their progress was very slow. The delay gave time for additional Union troops to reach Cape Girardeau. When the Confederates attacked the city on April 26, 1863, they quickly realized they could not capture the town. Once again, the southern raiders retreated to the area of Batesville, Arkansas.

In Pulaski County, the guerrilla raids, scouts, and small-scale skirmishes increased. One very annoying problem was the frequency with which the local stagecoach was robbed. The new commander of the Rolla District, Major General F. J. Herron, took a strong stand on this issue.

On May 1, 1863, Herron issued the following proclamation:

To the Citizens of Pulaski County Missouri:

The stage on the route from Rolla to Springfield having been robbed three times within the past week at or near the California House and the mails abstracted therefrom, the undersigned hereby gives notice, that he will hold the citizens along the route responsible for these acts.

First, that in the future any horse stolen will be replaced at once by stock taken from citizens in the vicinity.

Second, that any and every one captured who has been connected with these robberies will be shot without ceremony.

Without the citizens take measures to rid their neighborhood of these thieves, a very summary mode will be adopted to correct this matter.

In general, the summer of 1863 was a quiet one for the members of the Fifth Cavalry, Missouri State Militia, stationed at Waynesville. The routine duties of escorting a supply train, or scouting for signs of bushwhackers did not produce much excitement. However, their life was not exactly dull.

On the evening of June 19, 1863, Captain Josiah C. Smith, Fifth MSM, and a small squad of eight men found twenty-six bushwhackers six miles from Waynesville. They made a quick attack and the bushwhackers scattered in all directions. In what CPT Smith described as a "general running free fight," the Union troops were able to take only one bushwhacker prisoner. This man gave his name as S. S. Tucker.

Under the rules of warfare during the early part of the Civil War, a prisoner could give his parole and be released. Under these rules, he was to return home and fight no more. However, this system of parole did not stand the test of war due to widespread cheating on both sides. Prison camps were soon found on both sides of the battle lines.

In this case, CPT Smith accepted the parole of S. S. Tucker, but kept his horse and equipment. A short time later, CPT Smith found out the man's real name was Benson Woods. Smith later reported that, "The parole is, of course, not valid."

Following this brush with the bushwhackers, Smith and his men made camp for the night. Leaving camp on the morning of June 20, 1863, Smith's group scouted the land between the "Robideaux (sic) and Gasconade to near the line of Laclede County." This day proved uneventful and they again camped.

On the 21st, the group was joined by Lieutenant C. C. Twyford, of the Fifth Missouri State Militia Cavalry, and seventeen of his men. The combined scout now numbered twenty-seven men. The group found the trail of a small band of bushwhackers and began

J. B. King

to follow them. However, darkness fell before they could catch up with the outlaws.

On the morning of the 22nd, they again started on their trail. CPT Smith set a fast pace to make up for lost time. It paid off about noon when the Union troops ran head-on into some bushwhackers. Smith ordered a charge. The bushwhackers were caught in a bad position. They were making a noon stop and their horses were grazing. The surprise charge caught them off guard.

The bushwhackers scattered. Two men mounted and fled. Three men ran into the brush. Smith's men were able to catch one of the men on horseback and took him prisoner. The other mounted man vanished. Of the three men on foot, two were able to escape. Their leader, a man identified as "Casey, the noted stage robber," was mortally wounded in a gun battle.

CPT Smith talked to Casey before he died. Smith was able to ascertain from the man the location of a camp containing sixty-four bushwhackers near the Arkansas state line. Casey also told Smith that the captured bushwhacker, a man named Frick, had killed another man named Sherwood, near the Gasconade River the week before.

On the morning of the 23rd, Smith's troop took up the trail of the two men who had escaped on foot. After tracking them twenty-five miles, they located the two men in Wright County. Both men were captured as they ran from a cave. From these men they learned of another bushwhacker camp nearby. When they approached that camp, they found other Union troops from the Lebanon area already there. The two Union forces destroyed a number of bushwhacker camps within several hundred yards of each other.

CPT Smith and his men were ready to take up another bushwhacker trail when a very heavy rain wiped out the tracks. While waiting for the rain to stop, Smith realized that his men and horses were very tired. In addition, his unit had a number of prisoners and a quantity of recovered loot in their possession. He gave the order to return to Waynesville.

In his written scout report, Captain Smith noted that his men had captured three bushwhackers, killed one outlaw, recaptured seven stolen horses, and one government mule. He also recovered four saddles, two rifles, and two revolvers. He recovered a quantity of clothing, boots, and shoes that had been stolen from Mr. Stith's store in Lebanon.

CPT Smith closed his report with a plea for more men to take on patrol:

If we had the men here to work with, we could effectually break up this bushwhacking business as we now know the country nearly as well as they.

On August 25, 1863, an escort of fourteen men who were returning from Lebanon to Waynesville were attacked by Rebels. The place of attack was four miles west of Waynesville. The action began when a group of Rebels captured Mr. Hugh McCoin and several soldiers who were with him. Several of the bushwhackers "traded" clothing with the Union soldiers. The disguised bushwhackers then located the fourteen-man escort returning to Waynesville. In a short fight, they killed one Union man and wounded another. After the attack, the Rebels ordered McCoin to haul the dead Union soldier into Waynesville.

Upon learning of the skirmish, the new Waynesville post commander, Major Waldemar Fischer, sent thirty-five men under Captain Muller toward the California House. He also sent fourteen more men in an unspecified direction in an attempt to get ahead of the bushwhackers.

MAJ Fischer's counterattack failed. Neither of the Union units were able to find the Rebels.

On September 11, 1863, Captain Richard Murphy, Fifth MSM, stationed at Houston, Missouri, received information that six guerrillas had just traveled past a point ten miles south of Houston. He sent Captain S. B. Richardson, with twenty men, in pursuit.

When he arrived at the residence where they had been seen, CPT Richardson found the Rebels had obtained supper and continued south. Richardson tracked the band for fifty-seven miles. With his horses very tired, Richardson ordered a halt for the night in a wooded area.

J. B. King

During the night, Richardson obtained information that one of the Rebels, Martin Dodds, had left the party and gone to Thomasville, Missouri. Another member of the group had become lost in the dense woods. The remaining four Rebels were camped a short distance ahead of his men.

CPT Richardson and his men pushed forward the next morning and surprised the Rebels, asleep in camp. The men tried to run and all four were shot down. Richardson's men killed three of the Rebels. These men were identified as: William Lingo of Waynesville, Lieutenant Obe Moss of Pulaski County, and Jacob Bottom. The fourth man, Oscar D. Blount, of St. Louis was taken prisoner.

In his written report, CPT Murphy called attention to the importance of the recovered property.

CPT Murphy wrote:

With these men were captured 11 horses, 2 of which were stage horses, and 3 taken from a wagon on the road near Rolla; 7 citizens saddles and 3 bridles, 1 of them belonging to the stage company; 32 pairs of men's shoes, 17 pairs of women's shoes, 2 bolts of domestic, 3 sacks of coffee, 1 United States newspaper bag, and 1 set of stage lines. This is the most important capture made in this county, and too much credit cannot be awarded Captain Richardson and these men for their perseverance in the pursuit of these outlaws.

CPT Murphy continued:

I have gained valuable information from the wounded man Blount. He gave me the names of those that harbor and feed them. Among these are Andy Hall, living close to Judge York's, and Purcell close to Licking. I also found that William Lingo had 13 horses and a great variety of other stolen property at the house of John King, close to the Arkansas line; and Lee Tilley, son of Tilley near Waynesville has also a number of horses and other property secreted in the vicinity. The horses and other property taken in this scout I will send to Rolla by next train, and by mail I will send you a complete statement of the wounded man Blount.

On September 13, 1863, the men of Companies C and M, Fifth MSM, were in action at Salem. Their enemy was, once again, COL Freeman. This action started with a fight on September 12th in which one Rebel was killed. The force under Freeman numbered between two hundred and three hundred men. The next morning Captain Levi. E. Wayback, the commander of the Fifth Cavalry MSM at Salem, started a pursuit of Freeman.

After three hours of hard riding, the federals caught up with Freeman. In that battle, fourteen more Rebels were killed. CPT Wayback captured twenty-four guns, five horses, and two mules. The Union side had four men wounded. In addition, a civilian who had voluntarily joined Company C was also wounded. The citizen was identified as Mr. Copeland.

On the national scene, President Lincoln mourned the death of his brother-in-law, Brigadier General Ben Hardin Helm, who was killed at the Battle of ChicRamauga on September 19, 1863. BG Helm was a Confederate.

On September 22, 1863, another Confederate, Joseph O. "Jo" Shelby led his force from Arkadelphia, Arkansas on another raid into Missouri. This raid lasted until late October and covered a large section of Missouri.

As the troops of Jo Shelby approached Missouri, President Lincoln sent a message to GEN John M. Schofield, the commander of the Department of Missouri.

On October 1, 1863, Lincoln told Schofield:

Your immediate duty, in regard to Missouri, now is to advance the efficiency of that establishment, and to so use it, as far as practicable, to compel the excited people there to leave one another alone.

The men of Shelby's unit moved north. Along their path occurred a succession of military fights. There was action at Neosho, Missouri, on October 4th. From there the trail continued north. There was action at Stockton and Greenfield. Next the fighting moved to Humansville, then Warsaw, Missouri. Shelby's men fought at Cole Camp, Tipton, Syracuse, and LaMine Bridge.

On October 11th, Shelby men captured Boonville. Next were attacks at Merrill's Crossing and Dug Ford, near Jonesborough, Missouri. The trail of victory ended on October 13th at Arrow Rock, Missouri, when the federals won.

The fighting continued. Shelby's men were in action at Scott's Ford, Cross Timber, Johnstown, Deer Creek, and Humansville. As Shelby continued south, there was action in Cedar County and later at Carthage.

At last, on October 26, 1863, Jo Shelby's forces were fighting, but this time in Johnson County, Arkansas. The raid into Missouri was over.

While the fast-moving Shelby roamed through Missouri, some members of the Waynesville post were moved north to intercept the Confederates. One company of the Fifth MSM held possession of the Osage River fords from "Brockman's to Linn Creek." A second company of the Fifth MSM held Cabell's Ford located ten miles above Linn Creek, Missouri. These actions to prevent the Rebels from crossing the Osage River occurred from October 7th to October 22, 1863. The men from the Waynesville post did not fight Shelby's men during the raid.

Chapter Eight

Skirmish at King's Farm

While MAJ Waldemar Fischer led two companies of the Fifth MSM north to fight Shelby's raiders, the remainder of the unit stayed home. Their fate was to be routine patrol and boring escort duty. The fate they expected was not what they experienced.

On the 25th day of October, 1863, 2LT Charles C. Twyford, Fifth Missouri State Militia Cavalry left the Union Army fort at Waynesville with a small patrol. His mission was to scout southwest from Waynesville in search of information about a man named Benjamin Moore. Moore had been reported killed or captured by Rebel forces.

The first day's travel was quiet and the patrol members camped for the night at a point some fifteen miles south of Waynesville. About three o'clock the next morning, the duty guard reported to 2LT Twyford that someone was trying to sneak up on the camp. Twyford and several others ran to the place where the guard had heard the noise. The noise was repeated and the guard shouted a challenge to "Halt!" The unknown persons in the dark answered with a volley of gunfire. Twyford's men returned the fire for a moment, and the men in the brush were heard to flee.

At dawn, Twyford concluded his command was no longer in danger. The guard who first reported the bushwhackers' approach had been struck in the chest by a bullet. Twyford sent him back to the Waynesville Fort with an escort of seven men.

With his group reduced to just seven men, 2LT Twyford continued on another ten miles and arrived at a farm owned by Hiram King. In talking with Hiram King, Twyford learned that Benjamin Moore

The Tilley Treasure

had been captured by Rebel forces. However, he had either escaped or had been released on parole.

With his mission now complete, 2LT Twyford decided to feed his horses and men. While dinner was cooking, Twyford suddenly noted the approach of some twenty to twenty-five bushwhackers. Although the Rebels had achieved complete surprise, 2LT Twyford's men were able to stop the first charge with rifle fire. The bushwhackers then spread out and completely surrounded the farm.

Cut off from escape, Twyford looked for a defense. In building his farm, Hiram King had constructed two log cabins for his family's use. There was a large main cabin and a smaller one next to it, with a five foot separation between the buildings. Some three hundred feet to the rear of the cabins, he had built a blacksmith shop and barn.

Twyford ordered his men to take cover in the small family cabin. Inside the cabin they found Hiram King and his family. By that time, the bushwhackers were pouring a steady rain of bullets into the building.

Twyford's men and the King family were now trapped.

J. B. King

Hiram King pleaded with Twyford to leave before his home was destroyed. Twyford responded by prying up the wooden floor. He forced the King family into the crawl space under the house where they would be safe from the gunfire.

As the afternoon passed, the Rebels made several charges on horseback, but were driven off. Then they tried a charge on foot and were again driven back. The Rebel commander evidently concluded that as long as Twyford's men had the solid protection of the log cabin he would lose the fight. The Rebels set fire to the main cabin.

With the cabins only five feet apart, flames from the roof on the main cabin soon jumped over to the roof of the small cabin. With his fort burning down over his head, Twyford estimated their chances for a quick dash to the blacksmith shop and "concluded to ask for terms of surrender. Saw from their number it was useless to contend against them."

THE SKIRMISH AT KING'S FARM. THE CONFEDERATES IN THE WOODS FORCED THE TRAPPED UNION MEN IN THE HOUSE TO SURRENDER LT. TWYFORD'S PATROL WAS A FAILURE. DRAWING BY SUSETTE MCCOUCH.

Twyford's men ran out a white flag. Twyford and his men were veterans of several other battles in the Pulaski County area against the bushwhackers. As they faced the immediate prospect of capture, they feared the worst.

In his patrol report, 2LT Twyford stated:

We burned all the papers that would give any of our names or identify us in any way; changed our names, company and regiment for the reason that the bushwhackers had often sworn and circulated the report in the country if Frank Mason, Michael Williams and Lt. Twyford should fall into their hands, they would burn or shoot them full of holes. We thought it best to assume fictitious names.

With the white flag waving and the house still burning, 2LT Twyford and the Rebel second in command, a Captain Bristoe, discussed terms of surrender. After CPT Bristoe gave his word of honor that Twyford and his men would be treated as prisoners of war, the Union unit surrendered at 3:00 p.m.

Although the Rebel force consisted mainly of enrolled Confederate troops under the command of Colonel Love, there were a large number of bushwhackers riding with the unit. The bushwhackers wanted to shoot the prisoners, but COL Love refused to let them.

After surrender, Twyford's men were stripped of weapons and uniform. They were given old clothing to wear and, "Colonel Love would not allow any unbecoming language used to us." Love's command, plus prisoners, then marched toward Waynesville and camped for the night some twelve miles west of town.

During that camp, the bushwhackers continued to question Twyford's men "very closely." At ten o' clock the next morning the camp broke up; some seventy-five bushwhackers left Love's command. Love's men marched toward Lebanon, Missouri, until three o' clock that afternoon. While they stopped to feed the horses, COL Love told 2LT Twyford that he would release the Union unit on parole.

COL Love released Twyford's men from custody. He sent them toward Lebanon. However, a short time later, COL Love discovered the band of bushwhackers had followed his unit all day.

Fearing for the safety of Twyford's unit, he ordered them returned to camp.

In camp, the bushwhackers swore to COL Love that the prisoners would never reach Waynesville alive. However, COL Love had other plans. He placed the bushwhackers under arrest and had them guarded while he sent Twyford's unit toward Lebanon with a large escort.

Despite all of COL Love's efforts, a small number of bushwhackers followed the prisoners all the way to Lebanon. Twyford's men reached the Union Army post at Lebanon after dark on October 28, 1863.

In his final report, 2LT Twyford quoted COL Love's statement that five Confederates were killed and four wounded during the fight. The losses in Twyford's unit consisted of the guard who was wounded the first night, and two Union horses shot. Other than the embarrassment of capture, 2LT Twyford's unit was very lucky throughout the scout.

Chapter Nine

Wartime in Pulaski County

The skirmish at King's farm was the last big event of 1863 in Pulaski County. The rest of the year was very quiet. During this peaceful period, COL Albert Sigel completed his yearly report on the condition of the Fifth Regiment of Cavalry, Missouri State Militia.

In his written report COL Sigel said:

The regiment is well supplied with camp and garrison equipage, in good order; has all the transportation allowed by orders and regulations to a cavalry regiment, in good order; hospital accommodations, such as are allowed for a regiment in the field, but which are found in many instances insufficient and poorly. Medicines are furnished according to the medical supply tables, which are measured out so scantily that the supply is not sufficient for the period for which these issues are made. The regiment has been free from any contagious diseases. The health of the regiment in general has been good since the organization of the regiment. The increase of the regiment since last consolidation is larger than the decrease by desertion and discharge for disability. The aggregate of the regiment at present is one thousand one hundred and nine. The regiment is well mounted; condition of the horses is as good as any mounted regiment in this department. The regiment has marched on an average since in service two hundred miles a month. The arms of the regiment are rather indifferent and of too many kinds. Eight companies have originally been armed with Austrian rifles, which is, in my estimation, a poor arm for a cavalryman in pursuit of guerrillas and bushwhackers.

We have six hundred and thirty-three Austrian rifles in the regiment, six hundred and thirty-three revolvers, three hundred and twenty sabres, twenty-five pistol carbines, two hundred and two pairs of holster pistols, and fifty cavalry musketoons. As the regiment has proven to be one of the best disciplined and effective in the field in this department, and as the arms with which the regiment is now equipped are kept in first rate order, the regiment is justly entitled to be uniformly armed with No. 1 cavalry arms, and I would therefore draw the attention of the Commanding General to this fact. To give a minute account of the many midnight marches, the numberless exciting chases after guerrillas and bushwhackers, and the fatigues and hardships undergone by the different companies of the regiment, would be impossible at present, as it would fill an octavo volume.

With the military situation well in hand at the start of 1864, the attention of most Missouri citizens focused on the civil government. The new year brought sudden changes to the political scene.

Throughout his tenure as governor of Missouri, Hamilton R. Gamble worked hard. In late 1863, Gamble broke his arm in an accident. While recovering from his injury, he slipped and fell on the capitol steps. The already injured arm took the force of this fall. Gamble moved to St. Louis for treatment. While in St. Louis, he contracted pneumonia. He died on January 31, 1864.

The Lieutenant Governor of Missouri, Willard P. Hall, assumed the office of governor. Hall immediately addressed the General Assembly and made it clear he would continue the policies of Gamble.

The month of January also saw changes in the Union Army command structure in Missouri. On January 16th, MG Samual R. Curtis was reassigned to the Department of Kansas. General William S. Rosecrans was given command of the Department of Missouri. GEN John M. Schofield was moved from the Department of Missouri to the Department of the Ohio. Schofield was moved because he was the center of a political battle between moderate and radical Union men.

The Confederates named a new commander for the District of Arkansas on March 16, 1864. The new man was GEN Sterling Price, the ex-commander of the Confederate Missouri State Guard. As Price took over his new job, the first order of business was to plan a large-scale invasion of Missouri.

The Union high command feared 1864 would be the deciding year in the battle for Missouri. It appeared the Confederacy was primed for one last great invasion of Missouri. The ranking officers in the Department of Missouri were at work on plans to defeat this invasion long before it started.

Despite all this, the ordinary soldier in Pulaski County must have thought that 1864 was going to be a super year. Suddenly, there was no fighting action anywhere. The first six months of 1864 were the quietest period in Pulaski County Civil War history. The men found army life could be very dull.

Since it was first established in 1862, the post at Waynesville played an important role in the bushwhacker war. By the early months of 1864, the post had established a series of routine duties. The men of the Fifth MSM were required to escort supply trains and scout for bushwhackers. Although these main duties took most of their time, other job assignments did occur. In order to get some idea of their daily life, examine the following special orders.

These daily post details cover a span of time from March 27th to May 16th 1864.

> *Special Order No. 115 March 27th A.D. 1864*
> *Captain Charles B. Maus Commanding Company E.*
> *You will detail Lt. Uriah Bates and fifteen men; Privates provided with 2 days rations to go on a scout March 27th A.D. 1864. Lieut. Bates will report at these Hd. Qrs. before starting for orders.*
> *By Order of Waldemar Fischer*
> *Major Commanding Post*

Julius H. Baushausen Lt. & A.A.

Special Order No. 116 March 27th A.D. 1864
Captain George Muller Commanding Company A.
You will detail 5 men report to Lieut. Bates Co. E. immediately provided with 2 days rations to go on a scout towards Gasconade to start immediately this A.M. March 27th A.D. 1864.
By Order of W. Fischer
Major Comdg. Post
Julius H. Baushausen Lt. & A.A.

Special Order No. 117 March 30th 1864
Captain Charles B. Maus Comdg. Co. E. You will detail 20 men provided with 2 days rations to escort Paymaster to Gasconade River. They will report to Lieut. M. Griesback Co. A. tomorrow morning March 31st 1864, to start soon the Paymaster arrives.
By Order of W. Fischer
Major Comdg. Post
J. H. Baushausen A. Adjutant

Special Order No. 118 March 30th · 1864
Captain George Muller Commanding Co. A.
You will detail private Peter Christer of your company to report to Doctor Alexander Fekete Assistant Surgeon, 5th Regiment of Cavalry M.S.M. for duty immediately.
By Order of W. Fischer
Major Comdg. Post
J. H. Baushausen A. Adjt.

Special Order No. 119 March 31st 1864
Capt. C. B. Maus Comdg. Co. E.
You will detail one Lieutenant and fifteen privates provided with four days rations to escort Waynesville post train to Rolla. They will start tomorrow morning April 1st 1864 at 7:30 o'clock.

J. B. King

By Order of W. Fischer
Major Commanding Post
J. H. Baushausen Lt. & A.A. Adjutant

Special Order No. 120 April 1st 1864
Capt. C. B. Maus Comdg. Co. E. You will detail one Non-Commissioned officer and ten men provided with 2 days rations to escort government train of 60 wagons en route to Springfield to Gasconade and report to the Comdg. Officer of that post. And return to Waynesville without delay. To start tomorrow morning April 2nd 1864.
By Order of W. Fischer
Major Comdg. Post
J. H. Baushausen A. & A.

Special Order No. 121 April 3rd 1864
Lieut. Owen Carrill Company B.
You will escort government train with ten men of your company to Rolla, provided with four days rations and report to the commanding officer of the post. You will also take in private Loney, a deserter from 12th Missouri Volunteers and turn him over to the Commanding Officer of the post at Rolla. To start tomorrow morning April 4th 1864 at 7 o'clock A.M.
By Order of W. Fischer
Major Comdg. Post
Julius H. Baushausen A. A.

Special Order No. 122 April 5th 1864
Captains C. B. Maus and George Muller
You will each turn over all surplus ordnance stores which you may have on hand to the ordnance officer at Rolla at once.
By Order of W. Fischer
Major Comdg. Post
J. H. Baushausen Lieut. and Alg. Adj.

Special Order No. 123 April 6th 1864
Lieut. Martin Griesback Co. A.

The Tilley Treasure

You will escort post train to Rolla provided with four days rations with 11 men of your company and report to the Commanding Officer at that place and return without unnecessary delay.
By Order of W. Fischer
Major Comdg. Post
J. H. Baushausen Lieut. & Act. Adjt.

Special Order No. 124 April 6th 1864
Capt. C. B. Maus Commanding Co. E.
You will detail 6 privates of your company with 4 days rations and forage, to go with (unreadable), the scout expert to report to these headquarters immediately.
By Order of W. Fischer
Major Comdg. Post
Julius Baushausen Lt. & Adjutant

Special Order No. 125 April 7th 1864
Lt. Uriah Bates Commanding Co. E.
You will escort the paymaster to Houston with a detachment of 15 men of companies H, B, and E., provided with 4 days rations and forage to start this date at 11 o' clock A.M. this day.
By Order of W. Fischer
Major Commanding Post
Julius Baushausen Lt. & Adj.

Special Order No. 126 April 9th 1864
Capt. Richard Murphy Commanding Co. B.
You will turn over all surplus ordnance stores which you may have on hand to the ordnance officer at Rolla at once.
By Order of W. Fischer
Major Commanding Post
Julius H. Baushausen Lt. & Post Adj.

Special Order No. 127 April 10th 1864
Capt. Richard Murphy Commanding Company B.

J. B. King

You will detail Lt. Owen Carrill and 12 men to escort Waynesville post train to Rolla provided with 4 days rations. They will start tomorrow morning April 11th 1864 and return without delay. The Lieutenant will report to these Headquarters for orders before starting at 7:30 o' clock.
By Order of W. Fischer
Major Commanding Post
Julius Baushausen Lt. & Adjutant

Special Order No. 128 April 11th 1864
Company Commanders will have their companies in readiness for general inspection tomorrow April 12th 1864 at 10 o'clock A.M. They will also have made out a company monthly return, including the amount of ammunition on hand. The kinds of arms on hand, unserviceable, caliber. The return to be handed to the inspector on the parade ground.
By Order of R. Murphy
Capt. Commanding Post
J. H. Baushausen Lt. & Acting Adjutant

Special Order No. 129 April 11th 1864
Capt. C. B. Maus Commanding Co. E.
You will detail one sergeant and 15 men provided with 2 days rations to escort government train of 80 wagons en route to Springfield to Gasconade and report to the Commanding Officer at that place there to be relieved and return without delay to their command.
By Order of R. Murphy
Capt. Commanding Post
J. H. Baushausen Lt. and A. A.

Special Order No. 130 April 12th 1864
Commanding Officer Co. B.
You will detail 8 men provided with 2 days rations to report to Lt. Bates Co. E to go on a scouting expedition. They will be ready immediately after dinner April 12th 1864.

By Order of R. Murphy
Capt. Commanding Post
J. H. Baushausen Lt. & A.A.

Special Order No. 131 April 13th 1864
Commanding Officer Co. B. You will detail one non-commissioned officer and 15 men provided with 2 days rations to escort government train of 20 wagons en route for Springfield to Gasconade and report to the Commanding Officer at that place and return without delay for Waynesville. They will also report to these Headquarters for orders before starting.
By Order of R. Murphy
Capt. Commanding Post
J. H. Baushausen Lt. & Adjutant

Special Order No. 132 April 16th 1864
Capt. C. B. Maus Commanding Co. E.
You will detail one sergeant and 5 privates provided with 2 days rations to escort General Hunt to Gasconade. They will start tomorrow morning April 17th at 7:00 o' clock A.M. They will also report to these Headquarters for orders before starting.
By Order of R. Murphy
Capt. Commanding Post
J. H. Baushausen Lt. & A.A.

Special Order No. 133 April 16th 1864
Capt. C. B. Maus Commanding Company E.
You will detail private T. H. Yahn of your command as hospital nurse. He will report to Dr. Alex Fekete immediately this date.
By Order of R. Murphy
Capt. Commanding Post
J. H. Baushausen Lt. & A.A.

Special Order No. 134 April 17th 1864

J. B. King

Commanding Officer Co. B.
You will detail one sergeant and 10 men provided with 2 days rations to escort government train to Big Piney. They will start tomorrow morning April 18th 1864 at 7:00 o' clock. They will also report to these Headquarters for orders before starting.
By Order of R. Murphy
Capt. Commanding Post
J. H. Baushausen Post Adjutant

Special Order No. 135 April 18th 1864
Lt. Martin Griesback Co. A.
You will proceed with a detachment from Co. A. and E of 15 men provided with 2 days rations to escort Paymaster Major Wilson to Rolla and report to the Commander of the post and return without unnecessary delay.
By Order of R. Murphy
Capt. Commanding Post
J. H. Baushausen Post Adjutant

Special Order No. 136 April 18th 1864
Commanding Officer Company B.
You will detail one sergeant and 10 men provided with 3 days rations to escort a government train to Rolla. They will report to these Headquarters for orders before starting. They will start tomorrow morning April 19th 1864 at 7:00 o' clock precisely. Also they will report to the Commanding Officer of the post and return without unnecessary delay.
By Order of R. Murphy
Capt. Commanding Post
J. H. Baushausen Post Adjutant

Special Order No. 137 April 20th 1864
Commanding Officer Co. E.
You will detail one corporal and 7 men provided with 3 days rations to escort post wagons out in the country to move

in a citizen. They will report to these Headquarters for orders tomorrow morning April 21st 1864 at 7:00 o' clock precisely.
By Order of R. Murphy
Capt. Commanding Post
J. H. Baushausen Post Adjutant

Special Order No. 138 April 22nd 1864
Lt. Owen Carrill Co. B.
You will proceed with 12 men from Co. B provided with 4 days rations to escort Waynesville post train to Rolla and report to the Commander of the post at Rolla. They will start tomorrow morning April 23rd 1864 at 7:00 o' clock and return without unnecessary delay.
By Order of R. Murphy
Capt. Commanding Post
J. H. Baushausen Post Adjutant

Special Order No. 139 April 22nd 1864
Capt. George Muller Commanding Co. A.
You will turn over all surplus ordnance and ordnance stores to the ordnance officer at Rolla that is in your possession at the earliest period.
By Order of R. Murphy
Capt. Commanding Post
J. H. Baushausen Post Adjutant

Special Order No. 140 April 22nd 1864
Commanding Officer Company B.
You will detail 5 men with 2 days rations to go on a scouting excursion. They will report to Capt. George Muller commanding Co. A immediately.
By Order of R. Murphy
Capt. Commanding Post
J. H. Baushausen Post Adjutant

Special Order No. 141

J. B. King

Does not appear on the record.

Special Order No. 142 April 22nd 1864
Commanding Officer Company E.
You will detail one corporal and 10 men provided with 3 days rations to escort government train of 60 wagons to Rolla and report to the Commander of the post. They will start tomorrow morning April 23rd at 7 o'clock precisely.
By Order of R. Murphy
Capt. Commanding Post
J. H. Baushausen Post Adjt

Special Order No. 143 April 23rd 1864
Commanding Officer Company A.
You will detail one sergeant and 10 men provided with 2 days rations to escort government train of 40 wagons en route to Springfield to Gasconade and report to the Commanding Officer at that place, there to be relieved and return back to Waynesville to their command without unnecessary delay. They will start tomorrow morning precisely at 7 o'clock April 24th 1864.
By Order of R. Murphy
Capt. Commanding Post
J. H. Baushausen Post Adjt.

Special Order No. 144 April 25th 1864
Company Commanders will have their horses appraised by three disinterested citizens immediately.
By Order of R. Murphy
Capt. Commanding Post
J. H. Baushausen Post Adjt.

Special Order No. 145 April 26th 1864
Commanding Officer Co. B.
You will detail one sergeant and 10 men provided with 3 days rations to escort government train of 40 wagons en route

for Springfield to Gasconade and report to the Commander at that place, there to be relieved. They will start tomorrow morning April 27th 1864 at 7 o'clock precisely.

By Order of R. Murphy
Capt. Commanding Post
J. H. Baushausen Post Adjt.

Special Order No. 146 April 27th 1864
Commanding Officer Company E.
You will detail Lieut. Bates and ten men provided with 4 days rations to escort Waynesville post train to Rolla and report to the Commander of the post, and return without delay. They will start tomorrow morning April 28th A.D. 1864 at 7 o' clock precisely. They will report to these Headquarters for orders before starting.

By Order of R. Murphy
Capt. Commanding Post
J. H. Baushausen Post Adjt.

Special Order No. 147 April 28th A.D. 1864
Capt. C. B. Maus Commanding Company E.
You will detail one sergeant and 10 men provided with 3 days rations to escort government train of wagons to Rolla and report to the Comdg. Officer of the post, and return without unnecessary delay. They will start tomorrow morning April 29th at 7 o'clock precisely.

By Order of R. Murphy
Capt. Commanding Post
J. H. Baushausen Post Adjt.

Special Order No. 148 April 29th 1864
Commanding Officer C. B. Maus
You will detail one sergeant and 10 men provided with 3 days rations to escort government train of 40 wagons to Rolla and report to the Commander of the post, and return

without unnecessary delay. They will start tomorrow morning at 7 o'clock precisely.
By Order of R. Murphy
Capt. Commanding Post
J. H. Baushausen Post Adjt.

Special Order No. 149 May 1st 1864
Captain George Muller Commanding Co. A.
You will detail one sergeant and 10 men provided with 3 days rations to escort government train of 40 wagons to Rolla. And report to the Commander of the post, and return to their command without unnecessary delay. They will report to these Headquarters for orders before starting tomorrow morning May 1st 1864 at 7 o'clock precisely.
By Order of R. Murphy
Capt. Commanding Post
J. H. Baushausen Post Adjt.

Special Order No. 150 May 4th 1864
Commanding Officer Company E.
You will detail one sergeant and 10 men provided with 3 days rations to escort government train to Rolla and report to the Commanding Officer of the post, and return without unnecessary delay. They will start tomorrow morning at 7 o'clock May 5th 1864.
By Order of R. Murphy
Capt. Commanding Post
J. H. Baushausen Post Adjt.

Special Order No. 151 May 5th 1864
A Court Martial will assemble at these Headquarters at 10 o'clock A.M. May 5th 1864 or as soon as practical for the trial of such persons as be brought before it. Detailed for the Court Martial Capt. C. B. Maus, Co. E, 5th Cav. M.S.M. Lt. Clark Keyser, Co. E, 9th Missouri Infantry Volunteers. H. O. Carrill, Co. B, 5th Cav. M.S.M.

*By Order of R. Murphy
Capt. Commanding Post
J. H. Baushausen Post Adjt.*

*Special Order No. 152 May 8th 1864
Commanding Officer Company B.*
You will detail one sergeant and 8 men provided with 3 days rations to escort government train of 80 wagons en route for Springfield, Mo. to Lebanon, Mo. and report to the Commanding Officer of the post there, to be relieved and return without unnecessary delay. They will start tomorrow morning May 8th at 7 o'clock precisely.
*By Order of R. Murphy
Capt. Commanding Post
J. H. Baushausen Post Adjutant*

*Special Order No. 153 May 9th 1864
Commanding Officer Company E.*
You will detail one sergeant and 8 men provided with 4 days rations to escort Waynesville post train to Rolla and report to the Commanding Officer of the post and return without delay. They will start tomorrow morning May 9th 1864 at 7 o'clock precisely.
*By Order of R. Murphy
Capt. Commanding Post
J. H. Baushausen Post Adjt.*

*Special Order from St. Louis May 7th 1864
Leave of absence is hereby granted to Captain Richard Murphy, Company B, 5th Cav. M.S.M. for ten days.*
*By Command of Maj. Gen.
William S. Rosecrans
O. D. Green Adjt. Gen.*

Special Order No. 154 May 9th 1864

J. B. King

Company Commanders will have their companies in readiness for general inspection tomorrow morning May 10th 1864 precisely at 7:30 o'clock A.M. They will have made out an ordnance statement stating kind of guns, No. deficient, No. unserviceable, also kind of ammunition and amount of ammunition on hand will be given.
By Order of J. B. Kaiser
Major Commanding Post
J. H. Baushausen Post Adjt.

Special Order No. 155 May 10th 1864
In accordance to a request of 1st Lieut. Clark Keyser, 2nd Lieut. J. R. Roberts is permitted to proceed to Rolla to settle some business concerning the company.
By Order of J. B. Kaiser
Major Commanding Post
J. H. Baushausen Post Adjt.

Special Order No. 156 May 10th 1864
Capt. C. B. Maus Commanding Co. E. 5th Cav. M.S.M You will detail one sergeant and 10 men provided with 2 days rations to escort Colonel Sigel to Rolla and report to the Commanding Officer of the post, and return without unnecessary delay. They will start tomorrow morning May 11th 1864 at 7:30 o'clock precisely.
By Order of J. B. Kaiser
Major Commanding Post
J. H. Baushausen Post Adjt.

Special Order No. 157 May 14th 1864
Commanding Officer Company B.
You will detail one sergeant and 10 men provided with 3 days rations to escort government train of 40 wagons to Rolla and report to the Commanding Officer of the post and return without unnecessary delay. They will start tomorrow morning May 14th 1864 at 6 o'clock precisely.

By Order of J. B. Kaiser
Maj. Commanding Post
J. H. Baushausen Post Adjt.

Special Order No. 158 May 14th 1864
Commanding Co. E, 5th Cav. M.S.M.
You will detail one sergeant and 8 men provided with 3 days rations to escort government train of 40 wagons to Rolla and report to the Commanding Officer of the post and return without unnecessary delay. They will start tomorrow morning May 14th 1864 at 6 o'clock precisely.
By Order of J. B. Kaiser
Maj. Commanding Post
J. H. Baushausen Post Adjt.

Special Order No. 159 May 14th 1864
Commanding Officer Co. B.
You will detail one sergeant and 10 men provided with 4 days rations to escort government train of 40 wagons en route for Springfield to Lebanon, Mo. and report there to be relieved and return without unnecessary delay. They will start tomorrow morning May 15th 1864 at 6 o'clock precisely.
By Order of J. B. Kaiser
Major Commanding Post
J. H. Baushausen Post Adjt.

Special Order No. 160 May 15th 1864
Commanding Officer Company B.
You will detail one sergeant and 10 men provided with 3 days rations to escort government train to Rolla and report to the Commanding Officer of the post. They will start tomorrow morning May 16th 1864 at 7 o'clock precisely and return without unnecessary delay.
By Order of J. B. Kaiser
Major Commanding Post
J. H. Baushausen Post Adjt.

J. B. King

Special Order No. 161 May 16th 1864
Capt. C. B. Maus Comdg. Co. E.
You will detail Lieut. Bates of your command and one corporal that can write provided with 4 days rations to go to (unreadable} Missouri from thence to Miss Smith's after some beef cattle. They will start tomorrow morning May 17th 1864 at 7 o'clock precisely. Also the Lieut. will report to these Headquarters for orders before starting.
By Order of J. B. Kaiser
Major Commanding Post
J. H. Baushausen Post Adjt.

In July of 1864, a small Union Army unit left Camp Big Piney Missouri on a scout south toward Houston, Missouri. The group was under the command of Corporal Calvert, Fifth MSM. These men had orders to locate and capture "a noted bushwhacker by the name of Pruitt."

Other units had been unsuccessful in his capture. Calvert hoped to accomplish his mission because Pruitt had just robbed a Mr. Wayman, near Big Piney. Calvert's plan worked, Pruitt was captured. However, as the unit started back to Big Piney with the prisoner, one of the guards told Pruitt he was going to be escorted to Mr. Wayman for identification. Pruitt tried to escape. After a foot chase of several hundred yards, one of the guards fired a single shot. Pruitt died instantly.

The next day, July 6, 1864, a second scouting unit left Camp Big Piney Missouri. This unit, under Lieutenant Alfred Muntzell of Company F, Fifth Cavalry, Missouri State Militia, also went south. His scout went toward Johnson's Mill on the Big Piney. The unit repossessed one horse and one mule that had been stolen from the U.S. Army. Although LT Muntzell received numerous reports of Rebels between Spring Creek Hollow and Houston, Missouri, he failed to make contact with the enemy.

The men of the Fifth MSM at Camp Waynesville had a quiet month in August of 1864. The month of September proved to be a time of danger and hardship. Several important events occurred in Pulaski County; and Confederate GEN Sterling Price began an invasion of Missouri with twelve thousand troops.

The last invasion of Missouri by Confederate troops began on September 19, 1864. The plan of attack was to strike at St. Louis. Seizure of St. Louis would provide the Confederates with vast quantities of military supplies. GEN Price hoped to gain a large number of recruits from the St. Louis area population. If Union forces drove the Confederates from the town, the plan called for a fighting retreat across Missouri. The idea here was to go "through Kansas and the Indian Territory, sweeping the country of its mules, horses, cattle and military supplies."

Part of GEN Price's plan had political overtones. Riding with the army as a volunteer was Missouri's Confederate Governor, Thomas C. Reynolds. The Rebels hoped to seize Jefferson City and return the government of Reynolds to power. They felt the presence of Governor Reynolds in the capitol building would help resolve the position of Missouri's citizens.

The Southern column reached the area of Ironton, Missouri, on September 27, 1864. The town served as the Southern terminal for the railroad line to St. Louis. The town was protected by federal troops at nearby Fort Davidson. This fort had a very heavy defensive structure, with a large number of cannons and mortars. On September 27, approximately one thousand men under Union General Thomas Ewing waited for the Confederate attack.

When the attack did occur, the federals severely battered the Confederates. Union losses were described as "minimal," while the Confederates loss was more than a thousand men. With nightfall, the attack ended. In view of the large number of casualties, GEN Price paused to reconsider his plan of attack. Union GEN Ewing also considered the day's action and the thirteen thousand enemy still in front of his fort. Price elected to attack again. Ewing decided to get out while he could.

During the early morning hours of September 28th, the Union garrison evacuated the fort and fled toward St. Louis. The Union troops left behind a slow-burning fuse which destroyed the fort's powder magazine. The Confederates began a pursuit of Ewing's force.

As the Union force retreated, a Confederate division under GEN J. S. Marmaduke, moved into a blocking position between the federals and St. Louis. Unable to reach St. Louis, the outnumbered federals turned west toward Rolla.

On September 29th, the federals stopped running and built a hasty fort near Pilot Knob, Missouri. When the Confederates reached this new fort, they decided not to attack and moved north, they clashed with small Union units near Leasburg and Cuba, Missouri.

When GEN Marmaduke's cavalry rejoined the main body of GEN Price's troops, they found Price had abandoned the plan to attack St. Louis. As the two columns rejoined, small fights broke out near Richwoods, St. Clair, Union, and Washington, Missouri.

While the Confederate column was moving toward Rolla, the new commander of the Rolla District, General John McNeil, took severe steps to protect his command.

GEN McNeil wrote:

I issued General Order Number 35, District of Rolla, in which I declared Rolla a military camp. All male citizens of Rolla and adjacent country, including aliens and strangers temporarily present, were organized and placed under proper officers and set to work on the defenses of the place. This work was carried on day and night. On the 30th of September General Sanborn reported to me with between 1,500 and 1,600 mounted men. The same day I dispatched Colonel Beveridge with two battalions of the Seventeenth Illinois Cavalry as a reconnaissance party to Saint James and Steelville. That night, learning that General Ewing had arrived at Leasburg and was closely beleaguered by the enemy, I sent orders to Colonel Beveridge by special messenger to march immediately to General Ewing's relief. This order was most successfully executed by Colonel Beveridge and resulted in the safety of the toil worn force that had so far successfully retreated from Pilot Knob and their arrival at Rolla, some 700 men and six pieces of artillery being thus rescued from the very grasp of the enemy.

As the Confederate force moved farther to the north, GEN John McNeil reacted.

In describing his decision, McNeil wrote:

On the evening of the 3rd I became convinced that General Price was pushing for Jefferson City. All communication with St. Louis being cut off, I was compelled to act in the premises without consultation with headquarters. It also became known to me that one prominent object of the raid on the part of the enemy was the capture of the political capital of the state and installation of Thomas C. Reynolds as the constitutional governor of Missouri, and the inauguration of a civil government, that, with the assistance of this Rebel army of occupation, would be enabled to arouse the latent spirit of rebellion which still unfortunately existed in the minds of many citizens of Missouri. Determined if in my power to foil this Rebel scheme, I marched from Rolla for Jefferson City on the morning of the 4th of October, 1864, taking with me every effective man that a due regard for the safety of Rolla would permit. The force was composed of Seventeenth Illinois Cavalry, U.S. Volunteers, Colonel Beveridge commanding; Fifth Cavalry Missouri State Militia, Lieutenant-Colonel Eppstein commanding; one section Battery B., Second Missouri Artillery, Captain Sutter commanding; two sections Battery H, Second Missouri Artillery, Captain Montgomery commanding; one section 12-pounder mountain howitzers, Fifth Missouri State Militia, Lieutenant Hillerich.

GEN McNeil's men, plus artillery, and forty-six wagons marched rapidly north. They covered the seventy miles to Jefferson City in two days. Once in Jefferson City, his men worked thirty-six consecutive hours on the defensive line around the capitol. On the morning of October 7, 1864, the Confederates marched into sight of the capitol building.

Several small skirmishes occurred near the capitol and at Moreau Creek, east of Jefferson City. After a careful study of the capitol defense, GEN Price decided he could not risk an attack, and continued west.

On October 8th, another series of small battles were fought near Jefferson City. On the 9th, fighting occurred near Boonville, Russellville, and California. The Confederates continued west with the federals in pursuit. The Confederate force passed through Arrow Rock, Sedalia, Marshall, Glasgow, Waverly, Lexington, and Independence. They also attacked Danville, Paris, Ridgely, Smithville, and Carrollton, Missouri.

With the Confederates near Lexington, Missouri, the Union forces began to close the circle. GEN Price's military position was becoming unpleasant. His force was blocked to the north by the Missouri River. West of his location, Union MG S. R. Curtis waited with his Army of the Border. Approaching from the south was a strong infantry force, under General A. J. Smith. From the rear, the defending troops from Jefferson City were in pursuit.

The developing trap closed at Westport, Missouri, on October 23, 1864. Approximately 20,000 federal troops met Price's army in battle. Both sides had about fifteen-hundred men killed and wounded in this battle. Price's troops were forced to turn and head south. As the Confederates moved south with federal troops in close pursuit, a number of battles occurred along the route of travel.

The Confederate forces crossed the border into Kansas.

Fighting broke out at Marais des Cygnes and Mine Creek, Kansas. The march turned back east into Missouri. There was action at Reaveley, Carthage, Newtonia, and Pineville, Missouri. The end of October coincided with the end of Price's invasion. On November 1, 1864, the Confederates reached Cane Hill, Arkansas. The last major Confederate raid of the Civil War into Missouri was now history.

The campaign had been hard for the men of the Fifth Missouri State Militia stationed at Waynesville. In forty-eight days, the unit marched nearly eleven-hundred miles. The men of the Fifth MSM fought the Confederates at Jefferson City, California, Boonville, Lexington, Big Blue, Independence, and Hickman Mills, Missouri. In Kansas, they battled at Marais des Cygnes and Fort Scott.

The casualties for the Fifth MSM in these fights were listed as a total of four men killed and five wounded. However, on account of the over-exertion of their horses during the pursuit, about half of the unit's horses became unserviceable and had to be replaced. On November 15, 1864, the men of the Fifth MSM returned to Waynesville.

Upon arrival, they found out the small detachment left behind to protect the Waynesville fort had also been busy. On September 30, 1864, a small fight occurred in the town of Waynesville. On that date, Lieutenant Thomas B. Wright and members of Company B, Fifth MSM, attacked twenty guerrillas near the town square in Waynesville.

The guerrilla force had entered town without incident. They robbed the Pulaski County Clerk of $100.00 and took clothing from several citizens. Next, they moved to the fort and burned the horse stables used by one unit of the Fifth MSM.

In LT Wright's written report, he stated the Rebels set fire to the powder magazine inside the fort. The magazine did not burn. In the fight, LT Wright's men killed only one guerrilla. He was identified by citizens of Waynesville as the infamous guerrilla chief, "Bloody Bill" Anderson. Wright's men wounded two other guerrillas, but they escaped.

The dead Confederate was left where he fell for at least one day. The remaining Rebels sent word into Waynesville that if he was not buried, they would burn the town. Since all of the men were in Rolla at the Union fort, several unidentified women of Waynesville obtained shovels and dug his grave.

The burial may have occurred the morning of October 1, 1864. On that date, LT Wright informed his headquarters at Rolla that the guerrilla force was commanded by a man named Burkhart, from Texas County, Missouri. Although these men had told citizens of Waynesville that they were part of Confederate GEN Jo Shelby's unit, LT Wright reported several of the men had been recognized and were known to be bushwhackers.

J. B. King

In one respect, LT Wright was wrong. The guerrilla killed in Waynesville was not "Bloody Bill" Anderson. The real Bill Anderson was killed by Union troops in an ambush near Richmond, Missouri, on October 26, 1864.

In another small skirmish on November 1, 1864, Lieutenant D. W. Cantrell, Company G, Thirty-fourth Enrolled Missouri Militia, attacked a band of bushwhackers. This occurred "near the mouth of the Big Piney, at old man Black's." Cantrell reported a clash with four bushwhackers. His men wounded two of them and took one prisoner. On the way back, "The prisoner tried to escape, and the guard halted twice and then fired and killed him. I took two horses."

Chapter Ten

More Pulaski County Action

When the Fifth Regiment of Cavalry, Missouri State Militia, returned to Waynesville on November 15, 1864, LTC J. A. Eppstein re-deployed his force. He left Companies A, B, and H under MAJ John B. Kaiser at Waynesville. He sent CPT Maus and Company E to Big Piney. Eppstein sent Company F to Little Piney under Lieutenant Muntzell. Three companies moved to Rolla; G, K, and L under his own command. Lastly, he sent Major Newberry to Salem with Companies C, D, and M.

The last recorded skirmish of 1864 took place near Big Piney on December 2nd. MAJ John B. Kaiser, Fifth MSM, had sent a small detail to Big Piney looking for bushwhackers. His men killed three bushwhackers. The dead men were identified as Lewis Williams, I. S. Williams, and Levi Clark. MAJ Kaiser reported all three men were killed as they hid in a cave thirty miles southeast of Big Piney.

MAJ Kaiser reported all three dead men were deserters from Company C, Forty-eighth Infantry Missouri Volunteers. Besides having deserted from the Union Army, a search of I. S. Williams' body revealed a Confederate pass. According to this paper, all three men were members of Campbell's company of guerrillas. MAJ Kaiser reported a six-man scout he sent northeast from Waynesville had "succeeded in killing a bad character by the name of Charles Withers."

With 1864 coming to a close, LTC Eppstein sent a report to his headquarters regarding the year's activity.

A portion of Eppstein's report said:

Duties performed by the regiment were very excessive and hard, in the way of escorting and scouting, for which we have but little credit. The distance traveled by the regiment during the year may be safely put down at eight thousand miles. Notwithstanding these excessively hard duties, the effectiveness of the regiment is improving fast since the return from the late campaign. The sanitary condition of the regiment has been very good for the last year. Discipline is as good as can be desired. The officers and enlisted men in general have performed their arduous duties without grumbling.

The time of service of the regiment will soon expire, and as there are many good and deserving officers and enlisted men who should be retained for the service, I would recommend that they should not be forgotten when a chance for promotion offers. I should be glad to furnish a list of those most deserving any time when desired. The arms in possession of the regiment are in good condition. About three hundred Smith and Wesson's rifles have been purchased by the men, which is a very effective and desirable cavalry arm. The aggregate of the regiment on the 1st of January was eleven hundred and six, present aggregate seven hundred and fifty-two, showing a loss of three hundred and fifty-four, which was mostly on account of reenlistments into the 12th and 13th Missouri Cavalry, Volunteer Veterans.

With the beginning of 1865, most people realized the war would soon end. The massive federal armies were in the last stages of crushing the South. In Pulaski County, minor scouts and skirmishes continued to be a way of life for the men of the Fifth MSM.

On January 18th, Sergeant Hickman returned to Waynesville from Rolla with a supply train under escort. LT Bates reported killing two guerrillas near Big Piney on January 19th. The dead men were identified as McCourtney and Anthony. On January 20th, Sergeant Clawson returned from a hundred-mile scout up the Roubidoux Creek with nothing to report. On January 21st, CPT James Quinn led a detail to Rolla in order to escort the supply train back to Waynesville.

For some members of the Fifth MSM, January, 1865, must have been very welcome. Starting with COL Albert Sigel, several men of the unit were mustered out at the expiration of their term of service. Besides COL Sigel, those released included Lieutenant Martin Griesback, and all the men of Company A.

A SIMPLE REMINDER FROM THE PAST, A CANNONBALL FROM THE UNION ARMY POST AT WAYNESVILLE, MISSOURI. ALTHOUGH THE WAYNESVILLE CANNONS WERE FIRED FREQUENTLY FOR PRACTICE, NO RECORD EXISTS FOR THEIR USE IN COMBAT. PHOTOGRAPH BY AUTHOR

The month of February was quiet. The Waynesville post had only routine duty. The men of Company C at Salem were once again in the field chasing their elusive enemy, Colonel Freeman. Some fifty men, under Captain August Benz, conducted an extensive scout from Salem to the Arkansas line. They killed fifteen more of Freeman's men and captured twelve horses. CPT Benz reported COL Freeman was near Batesville, Arkansas, with on hundred men. The scout lasted from February 23 to March 2, 1865.

From March 5th through the 12th, MAJ John B. Kaiser sent a series of small details in several directions from Waynesville to search for a local citizen, Andrew Lawson. Mr. Lawson had been kidnapped by guerrillas eight miles north of Waynesville. Sometime near the 8th of March, the men of SGT S. B. Lewis' detail found Lawson's body near Houston, Missouri. Lawson had been shot to death. The detail covered one hundred-ffty miles in five days without success.

The Tilley Treasure

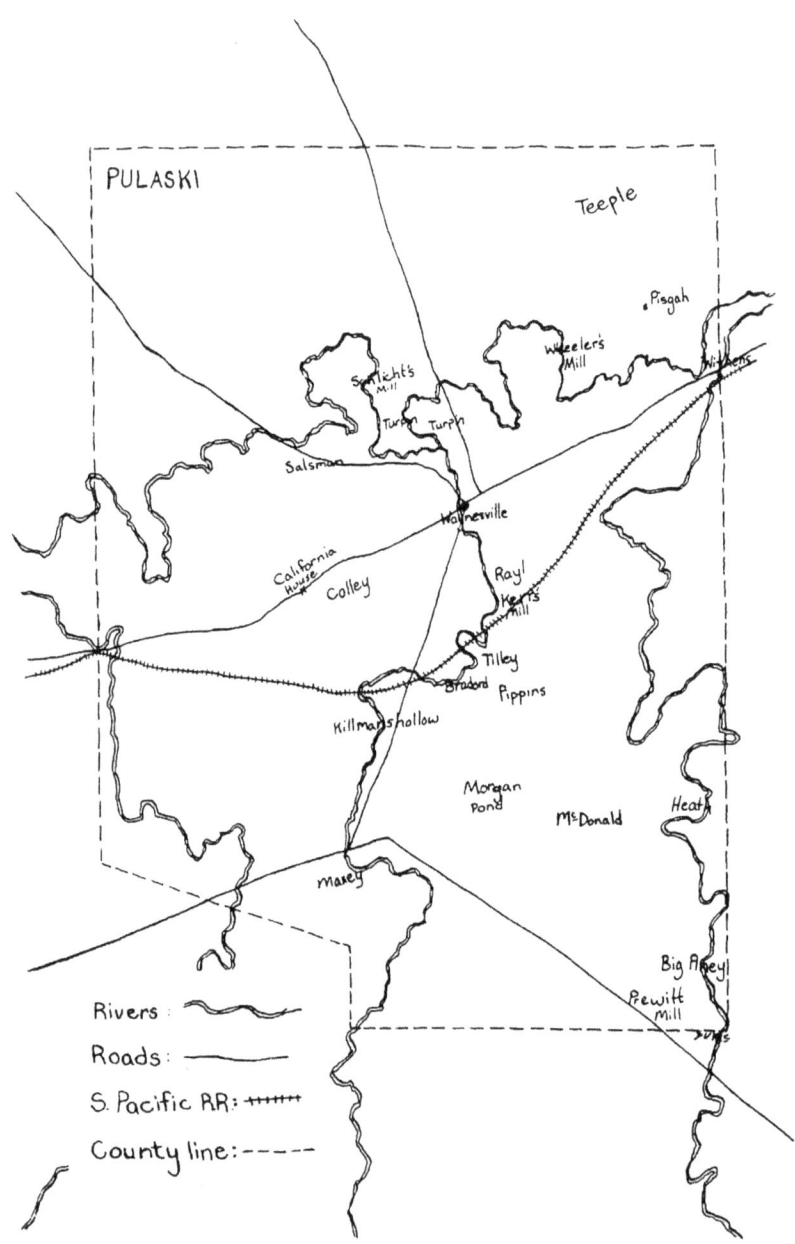

A Civil War map of Pulaski County. We have tried to pinpoint many of the locations referred to in the book on this map. The rail line shown was started before the war but was never completed. Drawing by Susette McCouch

J. B. King

On March 23, 1865, Sergeant John Y. Baldwin and six members of Company E, Fifth MSM, from Waynesville were detailed to escort a supply train. The detail picked up the supply train at Rolla and started west on the Springfield Road. At a point seven miles west of Rolla, they stopped for water at the home of Widow Yowell.

While SGT Baldwin and two men entered the home, the other four sat beside the road. At that time, five men dressed in federal uniforms rode up on horseback. These men drew revolvers and demanded the surrender of the four confused Union soldiers. The Union men gave up.

Then three of the disguised bushwhackers rode up to the house. They demanded the surrender of the rest of Baldwin's detail. The trapped Union men refused. They came out shooting. Their sudden charge surprised the bushwhackers. During the gunfight, the captured Union men were caught in a crossfire. After a second bushwhacker was shot down by SGT Baldwin, the remaining bushwhackers and the Union prisoners began running in all directions. SGT Baldwin reported two of his men, George Hoffman and John C. Odle, were wounded. One of his men disappeared. His fate was unknown.

March of 1865 marked the departure from the Union Army for most of the members of Company D and part of Company E, Fifth Regiment of Cavalry, Missouri State Militia.

During the last few days of March, 1865, the Waynesville Fort received a new commander. He was Major James M. Turley of the Thirteenth Missouri Cavalry. While enroute to assume command, MAJ Turley conducted a scout from March 29 to April 2, 1865. His report of the patrol was disappointing.

MAJ Turley wrote,

The roads were almost impassable on account of quicksand. April 2, I moved for Waynesville, swam Big Piney, and arrived here at 2 p.m., having seen nothing but quicksand and water on my way.

In April of 1865, almost all of the remaining men of the Fifth MSM were mustered out of the army at the expiration of their service term. The exception was a hundred new recruits, who were formed into a consolidated company. This company was commanded by Captain Henry W. Worth and Lieutenant Alfred Muntzell.

On the national scene, the month of April, 1865, was a time of victory for the Union. Confederate General Robert E. Lee surrendered his command at Appomattox Courthouse to Union General Ulysses S. Grant. The Civil War was not officially over, for Lee had surrendered only the Army of Northern Virginia. But for all intents and purposes, the war was over. The few scattered Confederate commands still free could not stand against the massive federal armies.

The evening of Good Friday, April 14, 1865, President Abraham Lincoln was assassinated by actor John Wilkes Booth. Lincoln was shot in the head as he sat in his box seat at Ford's Theatre in Washington. The shooting occurred just after 10 p.m. President Lincoln died at 7:22 a.m., April 15, 1865.

The surrender of Lee and the death of Lincoln did not end the war in Missouri. The Union troops at Waynesville continued to hear gunshots.

On May 14, 1865, Captain Richard Murphy led a detachment of Pulaski and Texas County Militia into action near the headwaters of the Little Piney River. In two small related fights, the Union forces clashed with bushwhackers. In the second fight, two guerrillas were killed and thirty others fled toward Hartville.

The date of May 23, 1865, was a proud day in the history of our nation's capital. The armies of the Republic marched through Washington in a last review. The Civil War was over. This grand victory march was the final proof.

However, there were a few folks who did not understand that the war was over. One of the last recorded skirmishes of the Civil War occurred on that same date, May 23, 1865. The place was ten miles northwest of Waynesville, Missouri. Lieutenant Uriah Bates, with a small detail of men, clashed with Dick Watson's band of bushwhackers. They killed two of the bushwhackers and captured three of their horses.

Following LT Bates' fight, the early summer months of 1865 must have passed very slowly for the men left in the Consolidated

J. B. King

Company, Fifth MSM. At last, in accordance with instructions from the War Department dated June 23, 1865, the Consolidated Company was mustered out on July 8, 1865. The Waynesville Fort was abandoned. The Civil War in Pulaski County was now over. There were no soldiers left to fight.

Chapter Eleven

The Death of Wilson M. Tilley

The legend of the Tilley treasure and the death of Wilson M. Tilley has been published many times. No two stories agree on the facts. The only common ground seems to be the fact that Tilley was killed for his money.

In the written history of the Waynesville Methodist Church, Tilley was reportedly shot by bushwhackers on an unknown date. In a second account in the Methodist history, Tilley was supposedly shot sometime in 1862. A third account in the Methodist history says he was shot in the last year of the war.

A newspaper article in the *Pulaski County Democrat* on December 6, 1962, says Tilley was shot in 1862. In the history book covering several area counties, published by Goodspeed Publishing Company in 1889, Tilley was reported shot by bushwhackers. In a story published in *Volume One* of the *Old Settlers Gazette*, Tilley was reported to have been hanged by federal troops. These troops killed Tilley after they discovered a side of beef in his smokehouse matched a side of beef in a nearby bushwhacker camp.

The true facts may never be known. The grave of Wilson Tilley can be found on Mark Twain National Forest land near the old Tilley homestead.

The gravestone reads:
Father-Wilson M. Tilley
Born June 27, 1807
Died September 10, 1864

The Tilley Treasure

THE GRAVE MARKER OF WILSON M. TILLEY. THE STONE CONTAINS THE WORDING, "FATHER, WILSON M. TILLEY, BORN JUNE 27, 1807. DIED SEPTEMBER 10, 1864. GONE BUT NOT FORGOTTEN."

One last account of Wilson Tilley's death comes from his great grandson, Joseph Newkirk Morgan. According to Mr. Morgan, Tilley was hanged by bushwhackers who were looking for his hidden money. Mr. Morgan says this occurred in 1864.

As Mr. Morgan tells the story,:

You see, this all happened the night Lee Hobbs was born. My grandma, Mary Ann (Tilley) Morgan, had gone up the valley to help her sister, Margaret (Tilley) Hobbs, who was about to deliver. Their mother, Elizabeth Tilley, wife of Wilson Tilley, had also gone to the Hobbs farm to help.

The next morning when Elizabeth Tilley returned home, she found her husband, Wilson, had been hung in a big tree near the house. The house had been burned to the ground. She buried her husband the next day. After the war, she dug up the gold they had buried and rebuilt the house. But Great Grandpa Wilson had not told her where the silver was hidden, and she could not find it.

You see, these were bad times. Why, the day after Grandpa Wilson was hanged by the bushwhackers, some more bushwhackers came upon my great uncle, George Morgan, while he was plowing in the field. Uncle George was only sixteen years old. He was plowing with a couple of steers, which were all they had left at the time. Uncle George had a little kid with him. Little Byron Ellis was only ten years old. Uncle George's father, John Morgan, had gone to the Union Army post at Rolla for protection. He left behind the women and Uncle George 'cause he thought they would be safe from the bushwhackers.

Well, these bushwhackers came up to Uncle George and decided to take him with them. They tied his hands and attached the other end of the rope to the saddle of a drunk bushwhacker. Then they started toward Waynesville.

I remember this well, for Uncle George told me this story many times while I was just a kid. Uncle George said he was just scared to death. He said when they reached the end of the field and started down into the Roubidoux Creek, he was able to untie his hands. He dropped down into the very tall buck-brush along the river bank.

Uncle George told me the drunk bushwhacker rode across the river before he discovered his prisoner missing. He then shouted to the other bushwhackers who had ridden on ahead. They all came back and began a search. Uncle George told me he could have reached out a half dozen times and touched their horses' legs while they were looking for him.

Uncle George told me that, after the bushwhackers left, he went back to the field and found the kid was still with the steers. They hid that night, and the next day Uncle George walked over the ridge to the Maxey farm. That night Uncle George and John Maxey, who was about fourteen years old, started to walk to the Union Army post at Rolla.

By the first morning, they had almost crossed most of Ft. Wood and had come out of Republican Hollow to where the Big Piney River Bridge crosses the Big Piney River. They waded across the river and hid all day in the brush. The next night they walked through Newburg and on into Rolla. Both of the boys stayed at Rolla until the war was over.

Yes, the Civil War times were hard. My grandma used to tell me how the soldiers would come in and camp in the yard. They would get hungry and kill a fat hog. They would eat and take only the best parts. After they left, Grandma would try to save what meat she could. They would also take whatever horse feed they needed.

Grandma used to tell me she was not afraid of the bushwhackers, but she was afraid of the army. Grandma said the bushwhackers were supposed to protect you. Grandma was not afraid of the bushwhackers even after they hanged Great Grandpa Wilson.

You see, Wilson Tilley was a mule trader. It ran in our family for a long time. Back then, some men rode mules, but most rode horses. They needed the mules to work with.

According to Mr. Morgan, Tilley's mule trade was quite extensive. He believes the buried money came from his sale of mules.

THE FIELD WHERE THE TREASURE WAS FOUND IN 1962. IN 1864, THE TILLEY HOMESTEAD STOOD IN THIS FIELD. WITH THE MURDER OF WILSON TILLEY AND THE BURNING OF HIS HOME IN 1864, THE COINS WERE DOOMED TO REMAIN HIDDEN UNDER THE RICH TOPSOIL FOR MANY YEARS. PHOTOGRAPH BY AUTHOR

As Mr. Morgan explained, there were no banks you could trust in those days. You had to keep your money at home. With armed bands of desperate men everywhere the ground was the safest hiding place.

It has already been noted that Wilson Tilley had troubles with the Union Army concerning the sale of mules. Mules were quite important during the war for transportation purposes. According to the Federal Census of 1860, there were 800,663 mules in the Confederate states, as opposed to 328,890 mules in the Union states. According to Mr. Morgan, just after the Civil War his family sold mules in the South for $75.00 each.

The Census of 1860 listed a total United States horse population of 6,115,458. The Southern states had 1,698,328 horses. At the start of the war a good horse sold for $125.00, but by the end of the war the price had jumped to $185.00. With figures like this, a degree of wealth could be expected for a livestock trader.

Just as an example of wartime use and loss of animals, consider a fight on September 19, 1864. The forces of Confederate Generals Stand Watie and Richard M. Gano successfully attacked a Union supply train in the Indian Territory. The Federal supply train was destroyed. The Union troops lost two hundred and two wagons, five ambulances, forty horses, and twelve hundred fifty-three mules. The value of the loss totaled one and a half million dollars.

Chapter Twelve

The Trial of Wilson Leroy Tilley

The conflict between the Tilley family and the Union Army continued to grow. On June 20, 1864, Wilson Leroy Tilley was arrested by federal troops near St. Louis. His traveling companion, Miss Emily Weaver, of Batesville, Arkansas, was also arrested. The Union Army thought they were spies.

Back on September 24, 1862, President Lincoln had issued a proclamation suspending the privilege of the writ of habeas corpus. Lincoln's proclamation provided for a trial before a military commission for "all Rebels and insurgents, their aiders and abettors within the United States, and all persons discouraging volunteer enlistments, resisting militia drafts, or guilty of any disloyal practice, affording comfort to Rebels against the authority of the United States."

This Presidential proclamation prevented Tilley from immediate bond. He was placed in the Gratiot Street Military Prison in St. Louis. On December 17, 1864, it appears Tilley was released from the prison. His release came as a result of Special Orders No. 321 from the office of the Provost Marshal General, Department of Missouri. As a condition of release, Tilley had to post a one thousand dollar bond, take an Oath of Allegiance, and report weekly to the Provost Marshal's office in St. Louis.

On February 10, 1865, case number 0.0.484, *United States vs. W. L. Tilley*, began in St. Louis, Missouri. The Commission was composed of the following officers:

Brig. Gen. S. A. Meredith, United States Volunteers
Brig. Gen. George H. Hall, Missouri State Militia
Col. W. A. Barstow, Third Wisconsin Cavalry Volunteers

Col. T. P. Herrick, Seventh Kansas Cavalry Volunteers
Capt. Wm. H. Judd, Thirty-first Missouri Infantry
Capt. L. Bulkley, Second Cavalry, Missouri State Militia
Judge Advocate; Lt. T. A. Post, Fortieth Missouri Infantry Volunteers.

The trial transcript begins as follows:

The Commission then proceeded to the trial of W. L. Tilley who was called before the Commission and having heard the order appointing the Commission read, was asked if he had any objection to any member present named in the order, to which he replied in negative. The Commission was then duly sworn by the Judge Advocate, and the Judge Advocate was duly sworn by the President of the Commission respectively in the presence of the prisoner.

The Reporter was also duly sworn by the Judge Advocate, in the presence of the prisoner.

The Prisoner here made application to introduce Counsel and Mr. Peacock and Mr. Cornwell were admitted as his Counsels.

The Prisoner was then duly arraigned, on the following Charges and Specifications which were read to him by the Judge Advocate:

CHARGE FIRST:
Violation of oath of allegiance.

SPECIFICATION: *In this, that he, W. L. Tilley, citizen of Missouri, did, on or about the Twenty-fifth day of August, 1862, take and subscribe an oath before an officer qualified to administer the same, whereby he bound himself to bear true allegiance to the United States, and support and sustain the Constitution and laws thereof, and afterward, on or about the twenty-fifth day of October, 1863, in the State of Missouri, violated said oath by joining and consorting and acting with enemies of the United States, at war therewith.*

J. B. King

CHARGE SECOND:
Being a guerrilla-marauder.

SPECIFICATION: In this, that he, W. L. Tilley, citizen of Missouri, did, on or about the Twenty-fifth day of October, 1863, unite, consort and act with rebel enemies of the United States, being military insurgents, bushwhackers and guerrilla-marauders, engaged in marauding and petty warfare against the United States.

To all of which charges and specifications the prisoner pleaded "Not Guilty."

At this point the Judge Advocate was ordered to call the first witness and the testimony in the trial of Tilley began. The following pages contain a complete record of the trial testimony.

You are now on the jury. Will your verdict agree with the Commission's?

TRIAL TRANSCRIPT
Testimony of C. C. Twyford, 2LT of Company H, Fifth Cavalry, Missouri State Militia a witness on the part of the prosecution, was duly sworn in, in the presence of the accused, and examined.

By the Judge Advocate
Q. Do you recognize the accused?
A. Yes sir.
Q. Did you see anything of him on or about the twenty-fifth of October, 1863?
A. I did on the twenty-sixth.
Q. Do you know of a certain capture being made on the twenty-sixth of October 1863?
A. Yes sir.
Q. State what you know about it.
*A. On the twenty-fifth of October I was ordered on a scout with fifteen men. We stopped at a place fifteen miles south of where we were stationed, the first night. That night

we were fired on by two men passing by and one of my men was wounded. The next morning I sent him in, with half of the men to Waynesville, and took the remainder of the men and went about eight or ten miles south of there and stopped for dinner. While getting ready for dinner, before we ate, I discovered a body of men riding on us. I saw they were rebels and we went into the house and stayed there some three hours firing at them. They found they could not get us out any other way, and they set fire to a house adjoining the one we were in. We then surrendered to them as prisoners of war on the twenty-sixth of October 1863.

Q. Is that all that occurred?

A. After we surrendered we were taken out in the road and our clothes, watches and everything was taken from us. I had asked Colonel Love, who seemed to be in command, on what terms we could surrender and he said we should be treated as prisoners of war. I asked him to give me his word of honor that we should be so treated, and he said he would. I recognize the accused as being in that squad of men who captured us.

Q. Did you have any conversation with the accused?

A. Yes, sir.

Q. State what it was.

A. I don't recollect the words that passed between us, but when first taken out in the lane and put under guard some of the men called for "Lee" three or four times, and afterwards added "Tilley" to it, and the accused went to them and was talking to them a few minutes, and then came to me and asked me if I noticed the remark they made. I told him I did, and then he told me his name and where he belonged and where he lived before going into that and all about it.

Q. Was that the same man you see here?

A. Yes, sir.

Q. To the best of your knowledge and belief what kind of men burned the house and captured you?

A. *From what Colonel Love told me himself, there were one hundred-fifty regular Southern soldiers and seventy-five bushwhackers.*

Q. *How long were they there?*

A. *About three hours before we surrendered.*

Q. *How long were you with them after your surrender?*

A. *We were taken in the evening, and were not released until next evening.*

Q. *Did you hear any conversations of the men at this time?*

A. *No, sir. Not any particular one.*

Q. *Was what Colonel Love told you in presence of the accused?*

A. *No, sir.*

Q. *Did you notice with what class of men the accused appeared to be most of the time?*

A. *Yes.*

Q. *State what.*

A. *He seemed to be with the bushwhackers.*

Q. *On what terms did he seem to be with them?*

A. *He appeared to be one of their commanders.*

Q. *Did you hear him give any commands?*

A. *No sir.*

Q. *How was the accused dressed?*

A. *I don't recollect.*

Q. *How were the bushwhackers dressed?*

A. *In all kinds of clothes. Some in federal uniform, some in gray, and some in citizen's clothing.*

Q. *Did the accused wear citizen's or military clothes?*

A. *Citizen's.*

Q. *How were the regular soldiers dressed?*

A. *Some were in uniform and some were not.*

Q. *How was Colonel Love dressed?*

A. *In citizens clothes, rather gray I think.*

Q. *What was the manner of the accused toward you?*

A. Very gentlemanly. He treated us with respect, and said he did not want to harm us.

Q. Did you see the accused at any time before he came up to you?

A. No, sir. I did not, and after we went into camp that night the bushwhackers, as represented by Colonel Love left and I did not see him after.

CROSS EXAMINATION
By the Accused

Q. All you know about the character of the troops was what you heard from Colonel Love?

A. Yes, sir.

Q. What was Colonel Love, a Confederate officer?

A. That is what he represented himself to be.

Q. All the men were under his charge?

A. He said one hundred-fifty of them were and that the others joined him as scouts.

Q. Were they under his orders?

A. I don't know. At least Colonel Love told me they were not.

Q. Was that in presence of the accused?

A. No, sir. Nothing was said in presence of the accused of the character of the troops.

Q. What did the accused do?

A. Nothing.

Q. Had he a sword?

A. No, sir. He had a revolver on.

Q. A revolver was all you saw him have?

A. Yes, sir.

Q. Did you hear him give any orders?

A. No, sir.

Q. He was not in uniform of any kind?

A. He had on citizen's clothes.

Q. Was there anything to distinguish him from a citizen but his side arms?

A. I don't know that there was.

Q. How many pistols had he?

A. I don't know whether he had more than one or not. I know he had one, and might have had more.

Q. You heard some men call him "Lee" and afterward add "Tilley" to it. State the circumstances of that calling. Were they calling for orders?

A. I don't know. He went to them, and talked to them.

Q. Did you hear the conversation?

A. No, sir. They were off fifteen or twenty yards.

Q. You say some of the men whom Colonel Love informed you were regulars were in uniform and some were not?

A. Yes, sir.

Q. Were those he said were bushwhackers and the others dressed differently?

A. I could not see any difference.

Q. How were those in uniform dressed?

A. Some had on gray and some citizen's clothes.

Q. Do you know whether or not they were formed into companies?

A. They were.

Q. Did you see them marching?

A. Yes, sir.

Q. Were those you designated as bushwhackers in companies?

A. No, sir.

Q. Did you see them march?

A. Yes, sir.

Q. How did they march?

A. Every way.

Q. Where did you see them march?

A. Where we went.

Q. Was your life in danger while in the hands of these troops?

A. I know some of them threatened it very strong, and all that hindered it was Colonel Love.

Q. Did the accused interfere to prevent harm to you?

A. I don't know that he did.

Q. While taking your clothing was any part of it reserved to you?

A. No, sir. They took everything, boots and all.

Q. Did you ever get anything back?

A. No, sir. We got some old worn out clothing.

Q. Who had you in charge? Those you understood to be regulars, or the others?

A. Colonel Love took us in charge.

Q. What character of troops guarded you, according to your understanding?

A. Colonel Love, after our clothing was taken from us.

Q. Who guarded you?

A. Colonel Love.

Q. You were under charge of Colonel Love then, at the time of your capture?

A. No, sir.

Q. Who captured you?

A. We fell in the hands of the bushwhackers in the first place. They were taking our clothing and wanted to kill us and Colonel Love came and took us away from them and put us under his men.

Q. Were these troops with Colonel Love at the time of your capture?

A. Yes, sir.

Q. They were part of his command?

A. Yes, sir.

Q. And Colonel Love guarded you?

A. Yes, sir.

J. B. King

Q. You were in charge of Colonel Love's troops then from the time you were captured until you were paroled?
A. No, sir.
Q. Were these troops under Colonel Love's command?
A. They were under his command while they were there and they left his command that night.
Q. Do you know whether they went away under orders or not?
A. They did not.
Q. How do you know?
A. Colonel Love told me so.
Q. When?
A. Before I was paroled.
Q. Was it in the presence of the accused?
A. No, sir.
Q. You only know then, from what Colonel Love told you?
A. No, sir.
Q. Did you hear him give them any orders?
A. No, sir.

The counsel for the accused stated that all statements made by Colonel Love to the witness as to the character of the accused, not in presence of the accused, or as to their going away without orders was not evidence.

RE-EXAMINATION:
By the Judge Advocate
Q. Did you or did you not hear any word of command given by Colonel Love to any troops at that time?
A. No, I did not hear a word 'til we were released.
Q. Did you hear him give any orders at all?
A. Yes, sir.
Q. State what they were.
A. After we were captured we were brought to within about twelve miles of Waynesville. The next morning, about one o'clock or later, we left that camp and started south toward

Mountain Store. We stopped at a stream and camped, and he sent out some men to get us something to eat. We had had nothing to eat since our capture. And he ordered Captain Bristoe, his adjutant, to write out our paroles.

Q. Did you hear any one call him colonel?

A. Yes, sir.

Q. What was his position while on the march?

A. Sometimes at the head of the column, and sometimes in the rear.

Q. Did he have the appearance and bearing of an officer?

A. Yes, sir. And all seemed to respect him, and all the men spoke of him as colonel. And, whenever he came around, all the officers and men seemed to respect him as such.

Q. Who gave the orders to march?

A. Colonel Love.

Q. Who gave the orders to halt?

A. Colonel Love.

Q. State to the best of your belief whether or not the accused was in command of those persons who were designated as bushwhackers?

A. I think he was.

Q. On the march were these men who were designated as bushwhackers marching all in a bunch or separate?

A. From the time we were captured until we camped they did not seem to be marching in any order at all, and they were not with us after the first night.

Q. While on the march, was the accused with the bushwhackers or the other troops?

A. I did not see him.

Q. Were you with the regulars?

A. Yes, sir.

The witness then retired.

ALLEN PARKER

J. B. King

Private of Company "H," Fifth Cavalry, Missouri State Militia, a witness on the part of the prosecution was duly sworn in presence of the accused, and examined.

By the Judge Advocate

Q. Do you recognize the accused?

A. Yes, sir.

Q. State where you were on or about the twenty-fifth of October, 1863?

A. We were up about King's. We were taken there by a party, and the accused was with them at the time.

Q. State all you know about that transaction.

A. We were captured there and taken off and paroled on the twenty-seventh, I believe.

Q. Did you see the accused at that time?

A. I saw him when first taken, after that I did not see him with the other party.

Q. What kind of a band of men was that?

A. I don't know, only from hearsay.

Q. How were they dressed and armed?

A. Some were dressed with citizen's clothes, and some with our clothes, and were armed with old guns and revolvers.

Q. What was the conduct of the accused, as far as you saw?

A. I don't know that he acted any way out of the way with us. He did not say much to us, only while the others were undressing us.

Q. What did he say?

A. He spoke to them and told them not to undress us there; he did not want to see us stripped.

Q. Was he present at that time?

A. Yes, sir.

Q. What did they do when they undressed you?

A. They took our clothes, and gave us their old ones.

Q. Who were the men who undressed you?

A. I did not know them.

Q. How were they dressed?

A. Some were in citizen's clothes, and some had old guns and revolvers.

Q. How long were you with these people?

A. I suppose we were taken about three o'clock and stayed with them until about sundown the next day.

Q. Who appeared to be in command of that party?

A. Colonel Love was in command of the main party, I believe.

Q. Do you know what was the position of the accused among the troops?

A. I do not, only from hearsay.

Q. Do you know how they addressed him in this company?

A. They called him Tilley, that is all I know.

The witness then retired.

HOWELL BRYANT

A citizen of Pulaski County Missouri aged 31 years, a farmer a witness on the part of the prosecution was duly sworn in presence of the accused, and examined.

By the Judge Advocate

Q. Do you know the accused?

A. Yes, sir.

Q. Where were you on the twenty-fifth of October, 1863?

A. I was on Roubidoux Creek, Pulaski County, Missouri.

Q. Did you see the accused at that time?

A. Yes, sir.

Q. State what you saw of him.

A. He helped capture me at that time.

Q. State what you saw, and all the circumstances as far as you saw the accused.

A. He was with a band of guerrillas.

Q. How do you know they were guerrillas?

A. By their actions.

Q. What did they do?

A. *After taking us, they stripped our clothing off of us and took everything we had.*

Q. *Was the accused present when the clothing was stripped off from you?*

A. *I did not see him.*

Q. *Was there anything else by which you judged they were guerrillas?*

A. *I think part of them were, and part were not.*

Q. *Did the accused say anything in your presence about that?*

A. *He said he was in a gang of bushwhackers.*

The accused objected to the foregoing answer as follows:

All statements by the accused are objected to upon the grounds:

1. That they are in the nature of confessions.

2. Confessions of accused must be made in open court to have any weight against him, and then they amount to a plea of guilty.

The commission was cleared for deliberation, and upon reopening it was announced that the objection was overruled.

Q. *Did he say anything else?*

A. *We wounded the man who was in command of the guerrillas and from the best information I could get, the accused then took command.*

CROSS EXAMINATION

By the Accused

Q. *Were you of the same body as Lieutenant Twyford?*

A. *I was with him.*

Q. *Were you captured by the same force he was?*

A. *Yes, sir.*

Q. *Was that commanded by Colonel Love?*

A. *He had command of some of them, sir.*

Q. *You say you don't know the character of the men except what was said, and you supposed they were guerrillas. What did they do that made you suppose so?*

A. By their stripping us of our clothing and taking our things, and the way they treated us.

Q. Is that all you saw?

A. No, sir.

Q. State what else.

A. Some of them called themselves so, and some did not.

Q. Did you ever hear the accused call himself a guerrilla?

A. Yes, sir.

Q. When?

A. At that time.

Q. How did he come to say so?

A. He said that was the party he belonged to.

Q. Is there any unfriendly feeling between you and the accused?

A. No, sir.

Q. How long have you known him?

A. Several years.

Q. Do you live in the same neighborhood?

A. No, sir. Within eight or ten miles of each other.

Q. Are you willing to state under oath that you have no prejudice against the accused?

A. Nothing more than his principles.

J. B. King

The trial of Wilson L. Tilley in St. Louis, Missouri forced a number of Pulaski County citizens to testify. Pictured is our idea of what the trial looked like as a witness testified in front of the Military Commission. Drawing by Susette McCouch

Q. Are you prejudiced from any cause against the accused?
A. I have none but that I consider him a Rebel and I am not, that is all.
Q. You state you have no prejudice against him except from principle.
A. Yes, sir.
Q. Are you a good loyal Union man?
A. I am.
Q. Have you always been so since this rebellion?
A. Yes, sir.
Q. Have you never sympathized with the South?
A. No, sir.
Q. You are willing to state you have always been a loyal man?
A. Yes, sir.
By the Judge Advocate
Q. What is the ground of your feeling toward him?
A. Because he is a Rebel.
The witness then retired.
The Judge Advocate announced that the prosecution here closed.

On motion the commission then adjourned until 10 o'clock A.M.

Monday, February 13, 1865.
St. Louis, Missouri
10 o'clock A.M.
February 13th 1865
The commission met pursuant to adjournment.

Present the same members as at the last session. (Except Col. William A. Barstow, Third Wisconsin Cavalry Volunteers - Sick.) The Judge Advocate, the accused and his counsel were also present.

The reading of the proceedings of the last session was dispensed with, the accused assenting thereto.

The accused then filed an affidavit (hereto annexed marked "A") asking for a continuance of the case until February 15th whereupon the Commission adjourned until the 17th day of February 1865.

St. Louis, Missouri
10 o'clock A.M.
February 17, 1865
The commission met pursuant to adjournment.

Present the same members as to the last session. (Except Col. William A. Barstow Third Wisconsin Cavalry Volunteers - Sick.)

The Judge Advocate, the accused and his counsel were also present.

On motion, the accused assenting thereto, the reading of the proceedings of the last session was dispensed with.

JOHN W. STEVENS
A resident of Rolla, Missouri. 30 years of age, attorney at law, a witness on the part of the defense was duly sworn in the presence of the accused and examined by the Judge Advocate, and examined.

By the Accused.

J. B. King

Q. Are you acquainted with the accused?

A. Yes.

Q. How long have you known him?

A. I have known him nearly a year.

Q. Will you fix the time of the commencement of your acquaintance with him, as near as you can?

A. I think it was some time in the early part of February 1864.

Q. Where was he residing at that time?

A. In Batesville, Arkansas.

Q. What official position did you hold?

A. I was Lieutenant Colonel commanding detachment of the Eleventh Cavalry Missouri Volunteers.

Q. Were you commander of the post there?

A. Not at that time. I was afterwards commander of the post in May and June.

Q. Was he residing there then?

A. Yes.

Q. At the time you first knew him, was he a citizen of Batesville?

A. Yes, engaged in business there.

Q. What business?

A. I don't know. I presume he was buying corn there, and that he was in business with Mr. Burr.

Q. Do you know whether the accused has ever taken the amnesty oath?

A. If he hadn't, he couldn't have remained in the town of Batesville. A short time after I assumed command of the post, by order of Colonel Livingston I issued an order that all persons who had not taken the amnesty oath and all persons who did not enroll themselves for the defense of the post and town within twenty-four hours after the promulgation of the order, would be required to leave then, and if they did not, they would be placed at work on the fortifications of the town. I haven't a list of these who enrolled themselves under that order, but I do know that at the time a great number, fifteen or twenty of the citizens of Batesville were ordered to leave in compliance with the order issued by me, I allowed no man to remain in Batesville that I did not consider loyal.

Q. If information reached you of any men who had not taken the amnesty oath and had failed to comply with your order what would have been your course?

A. I would have slapped him into jail at once.

Q. Did the accused remain in Batesville after that order?

A. Yes.

Q. Unmolested?

A. Unmolested by me.

Q. He remained then until you left?

A. I can't tell. The post was evacuated in June 1864 by order of Colonel Livingston.

Q. Will you state as nearly as you can the date of that order of yours?

A. It was June after I assumed command of the post, in May or June 1864.

Q. Then you say that all persons that were not loyal, who had not taken the amnesty oath, and who did not enroll themselves were required to leave?

A. Yes.

Q. And the accused remained there afterwards?

A. Yes. I will state that the provost marshal who was acting under my orders, was suddenly seized with sickness and died, and the business of the provost marshal office was thrown into confusion, and it fell to me to regulate it myself, and that a great many of the papers of the provost marshal office were lost, so that I could not tell who was enrolled. At the same time I exercised my discretion and banished the entire Weaver family, that is the young men.

Q. What was the size of the town of Batesville?

A. Probably two thousand.

Q. Was the accused a man of such prominence then that if he had not taken the oath, it would have been known?

A. I should think so.

Q. And his political sentiments, would they be known?

A. Yes, sir.

CROSS EXAMINATION

By the Judge Advocate

Q. Do you, or do you not know as a matter of fact whether the accused took the amnesty oath?

A. I cannot tell you.

Q. Might he not have failed to take it without you knowing it?

A. Yes, but not while I was in command of the post.

Q. Isn't it possible that he might not have taken it and still you not know it?

A. Yes.

By the Accused

Q. It isn't probable is it?

A. Yes. From the fact that it was professed before I assumed command of Batesville, and was in the charge of the provost marshal before I assumed office under Colonel Livingston, and he might have taken it then or he might not. I haven't access to the papers, and therefore I cannot say.

Q. What is your best information that he did or did not take the oath?

A. My best information is that he did take the oath, and I want to say this much more in justice to the accused, that he has at various times, while I was in command at Batesville given me very valuable information with regard to strengthening the post. And in various matters that I had under consideration for pursuing and harassing the enemy. I regarded him as a loyal man, and therefore I allowed him to remain there. He conducted himself as truly loyal as any man under my command.

By the Commission

Q. Can you state the terms of the order that you issued at Batesville with reference to persons taking this oath?

A. Yes. It was substantially in these words: All citizens of the town of Batesville should enroll themselves into a company of companies, the officers to be selected by themselves, and to be approved by me, for the defense of the town of Batesville, and those who refused or declined to enter these companies were to leave the precincts of the town within twenty-four hours after the promulgation of the order. The second clause required that no one should be enlisted or enrolled in these companies who had not taken the amnesty oath. The third section regarded the assessing of the companies, that the Quarter Master and commissary should furnish them with arms and rations while in service.

Q. Did this order provide for administering the amnesty oath?

A. No, it only applied to those who had enrolled. The provost marshal had charge of the enrollment, and they must enroll or leave town.

Q. Did any persons take the amnesty oath after the promulgation of this order, and in compliance with it?

A. Yes, sir. A good many of them.

Q. And these persons were also enrolled in the militia?

A. A great many of them were women. Not all of them.

Q. Then were some men?

A. Yes, I wouldn't allow any person to buy goods in the town of Batesville who had not taken the oath.

Q. Then your order required persons to take the amnesty oath as a condition of remaining in Batesville?

A. Yes.

Q. Did all those who enrolled have to take the amnesty oath?

A. No. There were a good many men who were regarded as loyal by us all, because they had belonged to the army before.

J. B. King

Q. If Tilley had come up and enrolled himself would you have required him to take the oath?

A. Yes, sir, I think I would. I always acted on the safest ground.

Q. And yet you say you considered him loyal?

A. Yes, but I should have taken the safest side, and if not positively certain I would have required the oath of him.

Q. Can you state the terms of the oath that was administered to these men, the amnesty oath?

A. It was in accordance with the President's proclamation. I have never given the subject my attention, and don't know the terms of it beyond that they should agree to abide by all proclamations that the President issued in regard to slavery.

Q. The oath that you speak of that you believe he took was the oath in obedience to your order?

A. Yes sir, I presume so.

Q. You didn't know of his taking it before that time?

A. I do not. I could not tell what occurred before my administration.

The witness then retired.

ADAM LEWIS (colored)

A resident of St. Louis, Missouri. 52 years of age, for the defense was duly sworn in the presence of the accused by the Judge Advocate, and examined.

By the Accused

Q. Do you know the accused?

A. Yes.

Q. How long have you known him?

A. I have known him since the last of August 1863.

Q. You may state where you knew him?

A. In Batesville, Arkansas.

Q. Had he lived there before that time?

A. No, sir.

Q. Did he come then to reside there?

A. Yes.

Q. What was his business?

A. He had a blacksmith shop.

Q. Was he carrying on the business then, blacksmithing?

A. Yes.

Q. Will you state how long you knew him to remain there?

A. He remained there from that time until I came away. I left him in Jackson post.

Q. When did you come away?

A. Somewhere near the last of May 1864, it was the time when the place was evacuated.

Q. Then you knew him to be there from the last of August 1863 until May 1864?

A. Yes.

Q. How often did you see him then?

A. I saw him sometimes three or four times a day, and sometimes once or twice a week.

Q. Did you see him as much as three or four times a week continuously?

A. Well, I saw him from the best of my knowledge once or twice a week ,or oftener.

Q. How far was your house from his blacksmith's shop?

A. About two blocks.

Q. Didn't his men board at your boarding house, some of them?

A. He did himself. He was every week at my house, and sometimes every day for two or three weeks, and then again once or twice a week. I hired his black man, one of them.

Q. Do you know what the amnesty oath is?

A. No.

Q. Do you know anything about the citizens of Batesville enrolling under the order of Colonel Stevens?

A. No, sir. I didn't know.

Q. In the Spring of 1864?

A. No, sir, I don't.

Q. Do you know whether they formed companies there?
A. Yes, I know about that. There were a great many of the citizens that did enlist then.
Q. Was the accused one of them?
A. Well, no. I don't think he was.
Q. Do you know whether he was or was not?
A. He was not.
Q. You know that of your own knowledge?
A. Yes.
Q. Did he remain there quietly pursuing his business?
A. Yes, trading there.

CROSS EXAMINATION
By the Judge Advocate
Q. You didn't know anything about the amnesty oath what it is?
A. No.
Q. You don't know whether the accused ever took the amnesty oath or not?
A. No, not by that name, I don't.
Q. What do you mean by that?
A. That is a word I don't understand, the amnesty oath.
Q. You say you don't understand what the amnesty oath is?
A. I do not.
Q. Then you don't know whether he took it or not?
A. No, sir.
The witness then retired

SAMUEL HIRSCH
A resident of St. Louis, Missouri. 35 years of age, merchant, a witness on the part of the defense, was duly sworn in the presence of the accused by the Judge Advocate, and examined.
By the Accused
Q. Do you know the accused?
A. Yes.

Q. How long have you known him?
A. About two or three years.
Q. Where did he live in the summer of 1863?
A. I think he was about Batesville, Arkansas.
Q. What was his business there?
A. I think he was currying in a blacksmith shop and trading in horses.
Q. How near did you live to him?
A. I lived about five or six houses from him.
Q. How long did he remain there in Batesville?
A. I don't know exactly.
Q. State as near as you can?
A. I left there a year ago myself and left him there.
Q. You left in February 1864?
A. I think I saw him there when I left, that was about a year ago.
Q. Had he been living there from the time you first knew him then?
A. He was about there.
Q. Carrying on his business?
A. Not when I left.
Q. Was he carrying on his business in the summer, fall and winter of 1863?
A. He was carrying on a shop a little while, I don't know how long.
Q. Can you state whether it was three months?
A. Well, I expect about that time, about that time, I reckon.
Q. What did he do afterwards?
A. I never saw him do anything myself.
Q. Was he still there?
A. He was still knocking about there.
Q. Do you know at what time he stopped carrying on his shop?
A. No, sir. I couldn't tell what month.

J. B. King

Q. Could you tell what time it was, whether it was near any festival or holiday?

A. It was late in the summer of 1863.

Q. When did he commence business in Batesville?

A. About 1863, I think.

Q. What time?

A. I think it was the latter part of summer, and then he was carrying it on two or three months.

Q. Do you mean in the summer months or in warm weather?

A. In warm weather... in September.

Q. How long did he carry on that business?

A. Maybe only a few weeks, maybe only a few months.

Q. Can you tell whether he did in November?

A. No. He did for some time, I can't tell whether two months or three months.

Q. Do you know that he was in Batesville from the time you first knew him until February when you left?

A. I knew him from that time on until I left.

Q. You lived, you say, only about five or six houses from him?

A. Yes.

CROSS EXAMINATION

By the Judge Advocate

Q. In October 1863, the accused might have been away from Batesville without your knowing it, might he not?

A. He might.

By the Accused

Q. You say he only lived five or six houses from you?

A. He kept a shop then, but he might have been gone without my knowing it.

Q. If he had been away, you would have been very apt to have known it?

A. I might have known it, but he may have been away without my knowing it.

Q. A week or ten days?
A. Yes.
Q. If he had been gone a very long time you would have known it?
A. Yes, a very long time.
Q. What do you mean by a long time?
A. Two or three months. He might have been gone a week, or two weeks without my knowing it.
Q. But not longer than that?
A. It might have been a week or three weeks without me knowing it.
By the Judge Advocate
Q. You don't know very much about him?
A. No.
The witness then retired.

JAMES CORNWELL

A resident of St. Louis, Missouri. 36 years of age, Lawyer a witness on the part of the defense, was duly sworn in the presence of the accused by the Judge Advocate, and examined.
By the Accused
Q. Do you know the accused?
A. I do.
Q. How long have you known him?
A. Since last July.
Q. Will you state the circumstances under which you became acquainted with him?
A. I think about June or July, Tilley was arrested with two others, one a Miss Weaver. We were retained for the defense of Tilley when his trial should take place. Miss Weaver was tried first by the military commission. I watched that case with a view to the defense of Tilley when his case should be tried. This was I think in August 1864 when the case was tried. I remember at that time amongst other papers which were there present, produced to be an amnesty oath taken by Tilley. I

had that paper in my hands, and I don't know whether I can remember the signature as Tilley's, but I am satisfied that it was his amnesty oath, and this paper was handed to Tilley at that time and he was asked the question whether it was his?

Q. What measures were taken by you to get possession of this amnesty oath, when and under what circumstances?

A. When these charges were preferred against the accused and we came in possession of them, I made an application to the provost marshal general to see all the papers in that case. I was refused, and asked if an order of the court would be sufficient, and that the papers would be produced on the day of trial. I spoke to Judge Advocate Post about it and he sent up for this paper, and I saw the return to the Judge Advocate that these were all the papers that they had. I think the note was signed by Major Eaton. I then made personal application to Major Eaton for these papers, and he told me he hadn't got them, that he didn't know where they were.

Q. What paper do you allude to?

A. The amnesty oath, I alluded to that particularly to Major Eaton.

Q. Where was that paper obtained?

A. Taken from the person of Tilley at the time of his arrest, of course I don't know that of my own knowledge.

Q. Did you ever see any papers that were alleged to be the papers taken from the person of the accused?

A. I did.

Q. I think you stated that you saw an amnesty oath?

A. I did.

Q. State your best recollection, information and belief whether that amnesty oath was the amnesty oath of the accused?

A. I believe it was. To my best recollection, I think it was the amnesty oath of Tilley, and signed by Tilley, and appeared to be recognized by the court as his amnesty oath.

Q. Do you know the date of it?

A. *I do not.*

Q. *Have you inquired of Major Eaton for this paper?*

A. *I have.*

Q. *What was his answer?*

Objected to by the Judge Advocate as irrelevant.

The court was cleared for deliberation, and upon reopening it was announced that the objection of the Judge Advocate was sustained.

Q. *Will you state what efforts you have made to get this paper?*

A. *I have applied to the provost marshal general and I was unsuccessful.*

Q. *Do you know whether this paper has been lost or not?*

A. *I don't know, I have not been successful in getting it.*

Q. *Have you reason to believe that the paper has been lost?*

A. *I presume it has been lost and can't be found.*

Q. *Do you know whether search has been made for it?*

A. *I believe search has been made for it. With regard to the letter from Major Eaton that I state what I saw, I saw it laying on the table here, stating that all the papers in his possession were forwarded at that time. The letter was not handed to me by any officer of this court.*

CROSS EXAMINATION

By the Judge Advocate

Q. *Why do you believe that the paper you saw was Tilley's amnesty oath?*

A. *From the impression on my mind.*

Q. *You have no knowledge of the fact?*

A. *Yes.*

Q. *What fact have you knowledge of?*

A. *The fact that I saw a paper purporting to be an amnesty oath in the hands of the Judge Advocate of the military commission, and the commission recognized it as such.*

Q. *Did you read the oath?*

A. *I don't think I did.*

Q. *Did you examine the signature to that oath?*

A. *I saw it, but I couldn't positively state that it was the handwriting of the accused.*

Q. *Did you notice when and where it was dated?*

A. *I did not, if I did I have no recollection of it now.*

Q. *You say that the court appeared to act upon it. What do you mean by that?*

A. *I remember that it was passed around the court and handed to Tilley, and he was asked if that was his, and whether it was his signature on his oath.*

Q. *But you don't know whether it was an amnesty oath or not?*

A. *I suppose it was.*

Q. *You didn't read it?*

A. *I don't remember whether I did or not, but from my impressions, I suppose I must have read it.*

Q. *Was it spoken of as the amnesty oath?*

A. *It was, and so recognized.*

The witness then retired.

T. A. POST

First Lieutenant, 40th Missouri Infantry Volunteers, Judge Advocate, a witness on the part of the defense, was duly sworn in the presence of the accused by the Presiding Officer of the commission, and examined.

By the Accused

Q. *Will you state whether you have in your possession a paper supporting to be the amnesty oath of the accused?*

A. *I have never seen such a paper in this office. I have looked for it, and have not found it.*

Q. *Have you ever made inquiry for such an oath at the office of the Judge Advocate of the Department?*

A. *I have sent out such a request, I believe.*

Q. *What was the reply?*

A. That there was no such paper there.

Q. Will you state whether the papers found on the person of a prisoner at the time of his arrest go into the Judge Advocate's hands?

A. I cannot state. I think they do not. Still, I don't know about that. My impression is that they go to the provost marshal and from there they come here.

Q. Have you ever made any inquiries at the provost marshal office for papers in this case?

A. I don't know, but the clerk may have sent for such papers, my impression is that there has been a note sent there.

Q. Is it the duty of the provost marshal general or his subordinate to forward to the court trying a prisoner all the papers affecting him?

A. I understand it to be his duty to do so.

ADAM LEWIS
Was recalled on motion by the commission and examined.
By the Commission
Q. Where were you in the Fall of 1863?
A. I was in Batesville.
Q. During the whole of the Fall?
A. Yes, sir.
Q. Did the accused live at Batesville during the fall of 1863?
A. Yes, sir. He was there.
Q. Was he there during the whole of that Fall?
A. Yes, I think he was there all the fall. In fact, he was there in September and I think in the last of August, I think it was, he carried on a shop at that time.
Q. What was he doing there after the first of September?
A. He was trading in horses and cotton.
Q. What time did he stop carrying on his shop?
A. It was some time in the winter, just a few days before Christmas when he quit, when the federals made a raid on them.

J. B. King

Q. Were the federals occupying Batesville during this time, the fall of 1863?

A. No, sir.

Q. They came in there about Christmas?

A. Yes, somewhere along about Christmas, it was.

Q. Was the accused there at the time the federals came in, about Christmas?

A. Yes.

Q. He remained there during the winter, did he?

A. Yes, he did.

Q. Was his business, all of it, at Batesville, in the town of Batesville?

A. No, sir. He was sometimes at Mr. Burr's about a mile or a mile and a half below Batesville.

Q. Was he in the habit of leaving the town and going about the country to do his trading?

A. Yes.

Q. How long would he be absent from town at a time?

A. I can't tell. To the best of my knowledge two or three days, and sometimes longer. I couldn't say exactly how long he would be gone. Sometimes two or three days, and maybe four or five days.

Q. And sometimes longer?

A. Yes, he was gone sometimes, I know. The way I came to know so well, he was at my house often. I kept a kind of a "meals at all hours" house, and all the gentlemen that wanted anything, something extra, they came to my house to get it. I laid in a great deal of that kind, and he came to my house to get refreshments of that sort.

Q. Was your business at your house?

A. Yes.

Q. That was where you were in the habit of meeting him?

A. Yes.

Q. Were you in the habit of seeing him at his shop?

A. Yes. I was there very often. I was a blacksmith myself, and that was the way I got acquainted with him. I called there to get my horses shod.

By the Judge Advocate

Q. Might he not have been gone a week or ten days or even longer at that time during the month of October, for all that you know about it?

A. To the best of my knowledge he might have been, from this fact that I was sick. I had lost my health from our heat in '62 when General Curtis was there and the greater part of my time for the last two years up to the winter of '63, and Spring of '64, I would be helpless in my bed for two months at a time so that I could not get out of my bed, and he might have been gone. But I very often would see him passing my house with the ladies. When I couldn't be up, and was in my bed.

Q. Can you mention a particular day in the month of October 1863, when you saw the accused?

A. No, sir, I cannot. If I could recollect the day that he broke the buggy in the mud hole at my house, I could tell, but I don't know whether that was in October or September.

CROSS EXAMINATION
By the Accused
Q. When did the accused come then to Batesville, first?
A. About the first of August, I first saw him.
Q. And he was in the blacksmithing business in September?
A. Yes.
Q. What kind of weather have you in Batesville in October?
A. Sometimes very fine weather.
Q. Is it cold or warm?
A. Warm.
Q. Now can't you fix from the character of the season, from the weather, can't you fix in your mind, and state positively to this court whether in the Fall of '63 you were confined to your bed for two months or not?

A. Well, I can. It was in '63. I was confined to my bed in the Fall, and in October too.

Q. How long in October were you confined to your bed?

A. I was taken down the second week in October.

Q. How long were you confined to your bed?

A. Three weeks at that time.

Q. Don't you know as a fact that during that time the accused was in Batesville?

A. I know positively that he was in my house, and he ate in my house in October, but what time in October I can't say. Our people usually have a great many peaches, and the accused bought a basket of peaches for Mrs. J M though I didn't go to the door myself, I saw him. I recollect that very well.

Q. That was in October 1863?

A. Yes.

Q. Do you recollect what part of October it was that you saw him buy the peaches?

A. No, I was in the bed, and didn't go to the door. My wife bought some at the same time.

Q. Do you know how long you had been in your bed when you saw him buying the peaches?

A. No, I could not tell.

Q. I understand you to say that you saw the accused on and off nearly every week until the place was evacuated?

A. Yes, sir, I did.

Q. You could often times tell when boarders were present at your house without seeing them by hearing their voices?

A. Yes, and my wife couldn't count the paper money, and she used to come to me to have it counted.

Q. Did you give the accused credit on your books for money so paid?

A. I didn't have any accounts. I did a cash business.

Q. Could you tell your boarders by their voices?

A. Yes, a great many of them.

Q. Would you know Tilley's voice when you heard it?

A. I don't know that I would. I don't think I would.

Q. Could you state to this court that you saw Tilley as much as once a week from September until the following Spring?

A. To the best of my knowledge I saw him once a week or three or four times a day, and then I wouldn't see him so often.

Q. Are you willing to state that you saw him to the best of your knowledge as often as once a week there?

A. Well, I just say what I said before. I believe I saw him as much as once or twice or three, or maybe more times a week to the best of my knowledge. I don't think there was any time when I was up and about, I saw him all the time, but when I was down sick, I don't know what occurred. I know I saw him once when I was sick, and I think I saw him more, but I couldn't be positive.

Q. His blacksmith's business was still going on then?
A. Yes.
Q. And he carried it on until just before Christmas?
A. Yes.
Q. Was he in partnership with Burr in September?
A. They were trading together.
Q. Were they still trading together in December?
A. I don't know. I know he was there.
Q. And you know he remained there during the winter, and along until late in the Spring?
A. He remained there until I came away.
The witness then retired.

H.A. VOELKNER

A resident of St. Louis, Missouri. 21 years of age. Clerk of the Commission, a witness on the part of the defense was duly sworn in the presence of the accused by the Judge Advocate, and examined.

By the Accused

Q. Will you state whether at the suggestion of the Judge Advocate you made inquiry for all the papers in this case from the provost marshal general?

A. *I did.*

Q. *What was the answer?*

A. *There was no answer. There was a package of papers sent and that is the package, (handing the papers to the accused.)*

The witness then retired.

The accused then offered in evidence the following endorsement upon the envelope containing the papers referred to by the last witness as follows:

Respectfully refused to Lt. Colonel Davis, a provost marshal general. There is no evidence in these papers to connect Tilley. I recommend that he be released on bond for future loyalty. He says he has taken the "Amnesty Oath." No farther oath can add thereto.

(signed) J. Warren Bell
Solicitor
December 17th, 1864

The Judge Advocate objected. The Commission was cleared for deliberation, and upon reopening it was announced that the objection of the Judge Advocate was sustained.

The accused then offered in evidence the paper hereto announced, marked B, which was admitted by the Judge Advocate to be a genuine instrument, and was there upon read to the Commission.

Upon the application of the accused for cause shown the Commission adjourned until 10 o'clock A.M. the 27th day of February 1865.

St. Louis, Missouri
10 o'clock A.M.
February 27th, 1865
The Commission met pursuant to adjournment.
Present the same members as at the last session.
The Judge Advocate, the accused and his counsel were also present.

On motion, the accused assenting thereto the reading of the proceedings of the last session was dispensed with.

SOLOMAN BARTLETT

2LT, Company A, 48th Mo. Inf. Vols., a witness on the part of the defense, was duly sworn in the presence of the accused by the Judge Advocate, and examined.

By the Accused

Q. Do you know Howell Bryant?

A. Yes, sir.

Q. How long have you known him?

A. For the last five years.

Q. Do you know his reputation for truth and veracity?

A. Yes, sir.

Q. What is it? Good or bad?

A. It is bad.

Q. From your knowledge of his reputation would you believe him under oath.

A. No, sir.

Q. Do you know what his political sentiments have been during this war?

A. I know at the beginning of the war it was said that he was a rebel, and he called himself that until our troops got possession there, and I suppose he calls himself Union now.

Q. From your knowledge of him suppose the rebels had been in power in Missouri would he have been Union or Rebel?

A. I don't think he is a man of any firmness. I think he goes according to the times. I have no doubt that he would have been a rebel.

Q. Do you know the distance between Batesville, Arkansas, and Waynesville, Missouri?

A. I think I know what it is generally called, but as to what the distance actually is I do not know. It is called two hundred fifty miles.

Q. Do you know the character of the country between these two places?

A. No, sir.

CROSS EXAMINATION
By the Judge Advocate
Q. How long have you known Bryant?
A. Five years.
Q. Have you known him intimately during that time?
A. Yes, I have been acquainted with him. He lived within three miles of me.
Q. How often did you see him, every day?
A. No, not every day.
Q. Have you known him within the last year or so to be guilty of any falsehood or dishonest transaction?
A. I don't to my certain knowledge. I couldn't say that I know of anything.
Q. Have you any reason to suppose yourself that if he were put on the witness stand he would perjure himself?
A. That is my belief about the man, and his general character, and his actions.
Q. What has he ever done?
A. In the first place he was a secessionist, and now claims to be a Union man.
Q. And that is the reason why you think he would swear falsely?
A. Yes, that and other reasons.
Q. What other reasons?
A. His dealings in the country.
Q. Mention one thing?
A. He won't pay a just debt if he can get around it.
Q. You infer from that that he wouldn't tell the truth on the witness stand?
A. The general character of the man is what I base my opinion upon.
Q. The only two reasons you can give for your opinion is that he has turned from a secessionist, and does not pay his just debts nothing more?

A. No, sir.

By the Accused

Q. If Bryant swore here that he had always been a Union man would that be a truth or a falsehood?

A. According to his say so, he was once a rebel, he might have been a Union man then, though he called himself a secessionist, but his actions didn't show him to be a Union man. I have heard him say himself that he was a secessionist.

Q. Do you know of any other instances?

A. No, sir.

Q. Do you know of his proposing to shoot Union soldiers?

A. Yes, sir.

By the Commission

Q. How do you know he proposed to do that?

A. I was in a store at Waynesville and a soldier that was taken prisoner at Wilson's Creek was in the house at the time, and he spoke about it, that they ought to go and take his arms. He had a revolver, the fellow did.

Q. What are your feelings towards this Bryant?

A. We never had any trouble in our lives.

Q. Did he owe you any money?

A. Yes, he owes me money now.

By the Judge Advocate

Q. Is there any ill feelings between you at all?

A. No.

Q. You entertain no ill feeling towards him?

A. No, nothing more than I never had any good feeling for any man who gets along in the way he does, but we have passed and re-passed.

Q. Still you don't like him?

A. I don't like his ways.

By the Accused

Q. But any dislike you may have towards him doesn't affect your swearing here?

A. No, sir.

By the Commission

Q. You have stated that you know what the reputation of the witness Bryant is for truth and veracity?

A. His reputation is the character he bears in his neighborhood.

Q. Have you heard it frequently spoken of?

A. Oh yes, by hundreds I reckon.

Q. In what sort of terms do they mention it?

A. They took upon him as being a dishonest man.

Q. You mean that, that is what they say about him?

A. Yes.

Q. What do they say about his speaking the truth?

A. They don't think him to speak the truth.

Q. Have you heard men give him the name of a liar?

A. Yes, sir, many a time.

By the Judge Advocate

Q. Do you recollect the names of any persons that you have heard speak about him in that way?

A. My captain is one, my first lieutenant is another, and he has a brother belonging to my company and he has but little confidence in him himself, I have heard him say so.

Q. Have you ever heard his veracity questioned in connection with anything else besides the payment of his debt?

A. Yes, I have in some other cases.

Q. On what other subject?

A. I don't know that there is anymore than what I have stated here before.

Q. Have you ever heard people express the opinion that he would tell a lie relating to any occurrence that had taken place, any ordinary occurrence, with no motive for doing so?

A. I don't know that I ever heard anyone say that, but I have heard them say they wouldn't believe him.

Q. How many people have you heard say that they wouldn't believe his word?

A. I have heard a good many. As I stated before maybe one hundred?

Q. You are confident that, that is his general reputation?
A. Yes that is his general reputation.
The witness then retired.

DAVID COLLIER

A resident of Rolla, Missouri, 27 years of age, physician, a witness on the part of the defense was duly sworn in the presence of the accused by the Judge Advocate, and examined.

By the Accused:
Q. Do you know Howell Bryant?
A. Yes, sir.
Q. How long have you known him?
A. Since January of 1862.
Q. Have you known him well since that time?
A. Yes.
Q. Do you know his reputation for truth and veracity?
A. Yes.
Q. What is it good or bad?
A. Bad.
Q. From your knowledge of his reputation would you believe him under oath?
A. No, sir.

CROSS EXAMINATION

By the Judge Advocate
Q. Have you known Bryant intimately?
A. Yes, sir.
Q. Have you know him intimately for two years past?
A. I have known him well since the Spring of 1862.
Q. Did you ever know during the last Spring of his being guilty of a falsehood or theft?
A. I don't know that I have only from the general reputation of the man.

J. B. King

Q. Did you ever hear anyone speak about his reputation in the years 1863, 1864, and 1865?

A. Yes sir.

Q. Mention the names of some persons that you heard speaking about him, say in 1864 and 1865?

A. I have heard Mr. Rayls, two of them, in the Forty-eighth Missouri: Lieutenant Bartlett, Mr. Mitchell. In fact, several in the vicinity of Waynesville.

Q. Do you know what they said about him?

A. They spoke of him as a man of no honor or truth, a man of no principle; generally a very bad man.

Q. And yet you have known him intimately during two years and can't think of anything he has done in the way of theft or lying in the last year?

A. I have been in Rolla during the last year.

Q. Then for all you know during the last year he has been an earnest and truthful man?

A. So far as I know of him personally. All I know of him during the last year is what I have heard.

Q. How about the year before that?

A. About the same thing.

Q. I understand you to say that you knew him intimately during the last two years, am I right?

A. Yes, I have known him since 1862.

Q. Intimately?

A. Yes sir, but for myself I have never had much business with Bryant. But, I have seen with him, and in the country that he lived in.

The witness then retired.

JAMES STORY

A resident of Waynesville of Pulaski County Missouri. 59 years of age, Farmer, a witness on the part of the defense, was duly sworn in the presence of the accused by the Judge Advocate, and examined.

By the Accused

Q. Do you know Howell Bryant?

A. Yes.

Q. How long have you known him?

A. Six or seven years. I live near him, within two miles of him.

Q. Do you know his general reputation for truth and veracity?

A. Yes.

Q. What is it? Good or bad?

A. It is bad.

Q. From your knowledge of his reputation, could you believe him under oath?

A. I couldn't sir.

Q. Do you know what his political sentiments have been during this rebellion?

A. I couldn't tell you. I heard him talk at the first commencement of the war.

Q. What did he say then?

A. He held up for the secessionist.

Q. If he swore on the stand that he had been a Union man all along, would that be the truth or a falsehood?

A. I think it would be false.

The witness then retired.

H. M. McKEE

A resident of St. Louis, Missouri. 45 years of age, trader, a witness on the part of the defense was duly sworn in the presence of the accused by the Judge Advocate, and examined.

By the Accused

Q. Do you know Howell Bryant?

A. I do.

Q. How long have you known him?

A. I have known him to the best of my recollection almost ten years. I will say eight, for certain.

Q. Do you know his general reputation for truth and veracity?

A. It is considered bad.

Q. From your knowledge of his reputation would you believe him under oath?

A. I would not.

Q. Do you know what his political sentiments have been during this rebellion?

A. I know at the breaking out of the rebellion he was the most uncompromising rebel that there was in the country; a perfect fanatic on that subject.

Q. If he states on this stand that he had always been a Union man, would that be the truth or a falsehood?

A. If we were to take his actions and his words to govern us, we would say it was a falsehood.

Q. Do you know the accused?

A. Yes.

Q. How long have you known him?

A. Thirteen years.

Q. Do you know his family?

A. Yes.

Q. Where do they reside?

A. In Pulaski County, Missouri.

Q. Do you know how many comprised that family at the breaking out of the rebellion?

A. I think I could count them up. Tilley's father, his two sons, and two young men that he had raised. That was the male portion of the family.

Q. What were the names of these two young men?

A. Vaughn, one Jasper L. Vaughn and the other Franklin Vaughn.

Q. As to Jasper L. Vaughn how long had he been living in that family?

A. I don't know. A long time.

Q. What was his relation to the accused?
A. First cousin.

Q. Was he known by any other name than that of Jasper Vaughn?
A. I have frequently heard him called Tilley.

Q. What was the "L" in his name?
A. Leroy.

Q. Was he called Jasper or Leroy?
A. I usually called him Jasper, I have heard him called both ways.

Q. Do you know how the accused was called?
A. We commonly called him Lee Tilley.

Q. Do you know whether this cousin of his was called the same name frequently?
A. I have heard him called so.

Q. Will you state who he resembled, if he resembled anybody?
A. Well Jasper Vaughn had a more striking resemblance to the accused here than his brother. His hair was nearly the same color, while his brother's hair was almost jet black.

Q. How was it about their ages?
A. He was some two years younger than the accused.

Q. How about this appearance of age?
A. There wasn't such a great deal of difference. I knew them when they were boys, and this one got grown sooner. After they both got their growth there wasn't so much difference in their appearance.

Q. Do you know whether Jasper Vaughn entered any military service? If so what?
A. I only know from general report that he entered the Confederate service.

Q. Do you know from report whose command he belonged to?
A. Colonel Love's.

CROSS EXAMINATION

Q. Who told you that J. L. Vaughn belonged to Love's command?

A. I don't know that. I couldn't identify any particular one, but it was the common report.

Q. You don't know anything about that yourself?

A. No, sir.

Q. Was the resemblance between Jasper Vaughn and the accused such that you would have confused their identity?

A. Both of them were school children of mine, and to me it was not difficult to tell them apart, but still there was something of a resemblance.

Q. Was it a very striking one?

A. It was about a common family resemblance. Persons would have taken them for brothers.

Q. Do you suppose that an observer would have mistaken one of them for the other?

A. I think such a thing might occur.

Q. Do you think it likely to occur?

A. Yes, I think it would be likely to occur.

Q. How long since you saw Jasper Vaughn?

A. Not since the breaking out of the rebellion.

Q. Four years ago?

A. Yes.

Q. How old was he then?

A. Perhaps twenty-two years old. Perhaps not that old; maybe twenty.

By the Commission

Q. Do you know where Jasper Vaughn has been during the last four years?

A. I don't know that I do.

Q. Do you know how close a resemblance there has been between these two persons within the last year or two?

A. I don't think there has been much change they were both full grown when I saw them last.

Q. When did you see them last, both of them?

A. Four years ago this coming summer.

Q. Was the resemblance greater or less then than it had been years before?

A. Greater, as they both became of age.

Q. Have you ever known any person to mistake Vaughn for the accused since they came to manhood?

A. I don't know that I have.

The witness then retired.

VIOLET LEWIS (colored)

A resident of St. Louis, 50 years of age, wife of Adam Lewis, (a former witness in this case) a witness on the part of the defense, was duly sworn in the presence of the accused by the Judge Advocate, and examined.

By the Accused

Q. Will you tell the court where you lived before you came to St. Louis?

A. In Batesville, Arkansas.

Q. How long did you live there?

A. I came there when I was a little girl.

Q. Do you know the accused?

A. Yes, sir.

Q. How long have you known him?

A. He came there I think in September, 1863.

Q. What was he doing when he was there?

A. He carried on a blacksmith's shop in company with Mr. Burr.

Q. How long did he remain there?

A. Until Colonel Livingston left. He came to Jackson post with the army.

Q. Do you recollect when your husband was taken sick in October 1863?

A. Yes it was along in October.

Q. Do you recollect what time in October?

A. I think it was the second week in October because Tilley was out there buying some peaches. He was there with the girls, and bought them some peaches and my husband was there in the room sick.

Q. How long after he was taken sick was it that Tilley was there buying peaches?

A. Almost a couple of weeks.

Q. Tilley came to your house frequently?

A. Yes, every two or three days. When he wasn't there, he was at Mr. Burr's. I used to see him riding with Mr. Burr's daughter.

Q. Do you know that he was there until Colonel Livingston left?

A. If he was away, I never missed him.

Q. He was at your house every two or three days?

A. Yes, every two or three days at my house regular.

Q. From the time you first knew him until the Union troops left?

A. Yes, a regular day boarder.

CROSS EXAMINATION
By the Judge Advocate
Q. Did he board at your house all the time?

A. Yes, except when he was down at Mr. Burr's, for two or three days, and then right back to my house again.

Q. Might he not have been away from your house a week or ten days October without your knowing it?

A. He could not have been away so long.

Q. Do you recollect whether or not he was at your house from the fifteenth to the twenty-fifth day of October?

A. Yes, sir.

Q. When was he at your house in that time?

A. He was there in October all the time while my husband was sick. I had to go in and get him to make change.

Q. Are you perfectly certain that he was at your house once between the fifteenth and twenty-fifth of October?

A. I couldn't tell the day, but from the time he came there he was there all the time eating.

Q. But you said he was at Mr. Burr's house?

A. Not more than two or three days at a time.

Q. Couldn't he have been away all the time between the fifteenth and twenty-fifth without your knowing it?

A. He couldn't have been out of town, for I saw him riding every day when he was at Mr. Burr's; riding with the girls.

Q. How do you know he was at Mr. Burr's at all?

A. I saw him riding with Miss Emma Burr.

Q. How many times was he at Burr's between the fifteenth and twenty-fifth of October?

A. He was every day or two riding with the girls, backwards and forwards.

Q. Do you recollect any particular time between the fifteenth and twenty-fifth when you saw him?

A. All I know is he was at my house and ate regular, from the time he first came in there.

Q. How was it from the twentieth to the end of October?

A. He was there, not every day, but every two or three days he was eating at my house.

Q. Do you know whether he was at your house on the twenty-fifth of October?

A. I couldn't say exactly on that day, but all along in October he was eating there regular.

Q. How on the twenty-sixth?

A. I never kept the days down, but what I say is he eat at my house regular all the time in October, at the time my husband laid sick.

Q. Do you recollect whether you saw him in your house on the twenty-sixth of October?

A. I couldn't say that day.

Q. Do you recollect whether he was in your house on the twenty-seventh?

A. I think he was, I know he was at my house.

Q. How do you come to know that?

A. I know he was, because I know he was there all the time.

Q. What did he do on the twenty-seventh of October?

A. He and the young men would come there and eat.

Q. Do you recollect him coming there to eat on the twenty-seventh of October?

A. I couldn't say he was precisely that day, not that day I couldn't.

Q. Then you say he was at your house on the twenty-seventh of October because he was a regular boarder at your house?

A. Yes.

By the Accused

Q. You know that from the time he came there until the Union troops left, he wasn't away from your place more than two or three days?

A. I never missed him away from my house, and when I didn't see him at my house, I saw him in the street.

Q. You remember about his buying the peaches in October?

A. Yes, sir.

By the Judge Advocate

Q. Have you had any connection with anyone in regard to your testimony here?

A. A man in the other room asked me what I was here for. I told him he would know when I was called to testify.

Q. Did you have any idea what you were to testify about?

A. No, sir.

Q. No idea what you were summoned for?

A. No, sir.

The witness then retired.

FRANK RILEY

A resident of St. Louis, Missouri, 29 years of age, substitute broker, a witness on the part of the defense, was duly sworn in the presence of the accused by the Judge Advocate, and examined.

By the Accused

Q. Do you know the accused?

A. Yes, sir.

Q. When did you become acquainted with him, and under what circumstances?

A. I arrested him, I believe some time near the end of last June.

Q. What was your position there?

A. I was a detective policeman here in St. Louis under Colonel Sanderson.

Q. United States policeman?

A. Yes.

Q. At the time you arrested him, did you search him?

A. I searched his trunks not his person.

Q. Did you find anything?

A. Yes, some papers.

Q. State to the court what those papers were?

A. I found several letters directed to people here in the city, and at Fond du Lac. I found some bills, and some oaths; two oaths.

Q. As to these oaths, what were they?

A. One was an oath of allegiance, and the other was an amnesty oath, I think.

Q. Give the dates of these, if you can?

A. One was in December, and the other in January; December '63 and January '64.

Q. By whom were they signed?

A. I can't recollect by whom they were signed. One was dated at Batesville, and the other at Little Rock.

Q. Who had taken the oaths?

A. Tilley.

Q. Are you sure that one was the amnesty oath?

A. I am, because of some remarks that were passed when I went to the office. I thought I had made a very important arrest. But when I overhauled his papers, and saw this oath, I thought all my labor was gone for nothing, because I thought they wouldn't do anything with him.

Q. Why did you think so?

A. Because I knew the amnesty oath shielded him.

CROSS EXAMINATION

By the Judge Advocate

Q. When was the amnesty oath dated?

A. In January, I think the oath of allegiance was the December oath.

Q. Do you recollect that?

A. Yes.

Q. And you recollect that Tilley signed it, the amnesty oath?

A. Yes.

Q. Where was it signed?

A. At Little Rock.

Q. Do you recollect anything in regard to the wording of it?

A. I cannot sir.

Q. Did you read it over?

A. Yes, I read it once. I can't recollect exactly the words of it.

Q. Have you frequently seen amnesty oaths?

A. I have not, I don't think I ever saw a copy of it before or since, except that I have read about it in the newspapers.

By the Commission

Q. How did you know that it was the amnesty oath?

A. From the fact that it was headed in such a style.

Q. What was the style of the heading?

A. This is to certify that W. L. Tilley took the amnesty oath. I made particular notice of that because what impressed my mind that it was the amnesty oath, was the remark that was passed at the provost marshal on it. We were talking about the arrest of him and Miss Weaver, and I remember saying that this was something of Lincoln's doings letting these men take this oath. I thought this oath would shield them, and we couldn't do anything with them at that time.

The witness then retired

JOHN W. STEVENS
Was recalled on the part of the defense, and examined.
By the Accused
Q. Do you know the distance from Batesville, Arkansas, to Waynesville, Missouri?
A. Yes, I think I do. I have traveled over the ground several times.
Q. How far is the distance?
A. By the most direct route, one hundred ninety-five miles.
Q. What is the character of the country between the two places?
A. A part way broken, and a part of it tolerably level.
Q. How long would it take to make a march between the two places, say for infantry in October?
A. Fifteen days to make the march between the two places.
Q. And fifteen days to return?
A. Yes, sir, for infantry.
The witness then retired.
With the end of Steven's testimony, the defense rested. The members of the Commission retired to deliberate their verdict. What verdict did you reach?

The verdict of the Commission was as follows:

FINDING:
The Commission, having maturely considered the evidence adduced, finds the prisoner as follows:
Of the specification, first charge, "Not Guilty."
Of the first charge, "Not Guilty."
Of the specification, second charge, "Guilty, except the words 'of Missouri.'"
Of the second charge, "Guilty."

SENTENCE:

J. B. King

And the Commission does therefore sentence him, W. L. Tilley, "to imprisonment during the war, at such place as the General commanding the Department shall designate."

Finding and sentence confirmed. The sentence will be carried into effect at the Military Prison at Alton, Illinois, under the direction of the Provost Marshal General.

Chapter Thirteen

Miss Emily Weaver

At the same time Tilley was arrested, the federal authorities arrested Miss Emily Weaver of Batesville, Arkansas. Her story adds drama to the Civil War. Unlike Tilley, she was tried on a charge of spying for the Confederacy. She was convicted and sentenced to "hang by the neck until dead." Miss Weaver was seventeen years old.

The transcript of Miss Weaver's trial runs over two hundred pages. Limitations on book space prohibit printing her complete record. Since her record applies to W. L. Tilley, her story should be covered in detail.

Following their arrest on June 20, 1864, Miss Weaver was placed in a military prison in St. Louis. Weaver and Tilley were taken into custody at a private home near St. Louis. The reason why federal authorities were watching this home was never explained.

During the early summer of 1864, the Union Army command in Missouri was very worried. The forthcoming invasion of Missouri by GEN Sterling Price would place a heavy burden on the Department of Missouri. Due to large-scale fighting in the East, the federal troop strength in Missouri had been cut. The Confederate's proposed capture of St. Louis was a serious threat.

The Union Army took immediate steps to lessen the flow of military intelligence to the Confederates. Travel in Missouri without a valid army pass became nearly impossible. The Provost Marshal's office increased the number of men looking for Confederate spies. Those men found Miss Weaver.

The trial of Emily Weaver began on August 2, 1864. The first person to testify was Frank Riley, a detective who helped arrest her.

The Tilley Treasure

Riley said that when he questioned Miss Weaver, she admitted being inside both Union and Southern lines within the past year. Riley identified for the court several letters, and a Confederate travel pass he seized from Tilley. Riley told the Commission he arrested the pair at Mrs. Mary Jane Lingo's home in Carondelet, Missouri. He spoke of a mystery man who made a brief visit to the home and vanished. Riley testified that Mrs. Lingo and her family were known for their Southern sympathy. He told the Commission how he followed the group as they traveled about St. Louis.

Next to speak was Mrs. Eleanor King, a resident of Rolla, Missouri. Mrs. King told the Commission she met Weaver in Batesville, Arkansas. King spoke of Weaver making a trip with her to Rolla. She denied seeing any high-ranking Confederate officers around Batesville. Mrs. King told the Commission her sympathy was with the South. She denied any knowledge of letters or military information being given to Miss Weaver. Mrs. King said that Mrs. Lingo had a Rebel son who was killed somewhere near the Missouri boundary line. She said Emily Weaver favored the South.

The next party to testify was W. L. Tilley. Under oath, Tilley said he had known Weaver for more than two years. Tilley said he had served in the Rebel Army and left it in 1861. Tilley told the Commission he had taken the Oath of Allegiance first in Pulaski County. He took a second oath in Batesville on December 23, 1863. He said he took the oath a third time at Little Rock.

According to Tilley, Confederate General Jo Shelby seized Batesville the same morning he (Tilley) left for St. Louis. Tilley denied getting the Confederate travel pass found in his valise. Tilley told the Commission that Mrs. Lingo favored the South. He stated Mrs. Lingo had a bushwhacker son killed near Salem, Missouri. He denied being present when William Lingo was buried.

Tilley denied any knowledge of a diary kept by Emily Weaver. He told the court she had spent two or three days in Pilot Knob, Missouri, while enroute to St. Louis. He also said he did not travel with her to Rolla, since he had to go into Illinois on some old business regarding the sale of horses.

The next person to testify was Laura B. Lingo, from Carondelet, Missouri. Miss Lingo told the Commission she first met Weaver at the Lindell Hotel in St. Louis in June of 1864. She had gone there to see her old Pulaski County neighbor, W. L. Tilley. Miss Lingo told the Commission Weaver had stayed at their house for three weeks. Lingo admitted going to Rolla with her. She also denied knowledge of Weaver's alleged diary. She told the Commission her Rebel brother had been killed in a skirmish. Lingo said Weaver had been warned the detectives were watching her, but she did not know who had warned her.

Miss Lingo told of a trip to visit a man named McKee, who was an old teacher of Tilley's. Mr. McKee operated a riding stable near St. Louis. Lingo said Miss Weaver carried a pistol with her.

Next to testify was Mrs. Mary Jane Lingo of Carondelet, Missouri. She told the Commission she had known Weaver about two months. She said Weaver and Tilley were arrested at her house. She spoke of the mystery man who warned Weaver that the detectives were watching her. She admitted the death of her son in the Rebel service. She did not know if Tilley was with him at the time. Mrs. Lingo said she had received a letter from W. L. Tilley in which he described her son's burial.

Mary Jane Lingo told the Commission that Weaver and her daughter had gone to visit Tilley's relatives in Rolla. She said Tilley did not go with them. (Mahala L. Tilley had married Dr. David Collier. They lived in Rolla.) Mrs. Lingo said she had no knowledge of troop movements, troop numbers, or positions of army forts. She also denied that her daughter and W. L. Tilley were engaged. She said they had been close friends since childhood.

Mrs. Lingo told the Commission that Weaver expected to meet some federal officers in St. Louis whom she had known in Batesville. She denied any knowledge that Weaver might know Confederate officers or of having visited Confederate headquarters in Batesville.

The next witness to testify was Miss Mary Ann Pittman from Tennessee. Miss Pittman told the Commission she met Weaver when Weaver became her cell mate at the female prison. According to Pittman, Weaver said she was a Rebel spy. Weaver also said the federals could not prove their case as they did not know what she had done. Weaver stated the federal case was up to a Lieutenant Dodge and she had him under her control.

According to Pittman, Weaver was afraid Tilley would hang, since his charges were very severe. Weaver said she had never met a federal officer she could not wind around her finger. Weaver told her she had been a spy for two years. She worked for General Shelby and was paid $75.00 per month.

Pittman said Weaver had been wearing a pair of gloves marked, "Col. E. W. Weaver, CSA" at the time of her arrest. She said Weaver's first action in the cell was to cut up the gloves and throw them in the fire. Pittman told the Commission she sent LT Dodge a note and he came to the cell and recovered the gloves from the fire. The gloves were offered into evidence after Pittman identified them.

Pittman said Weaver still had her pistol when put into the cell. Pittman said Weaver gave her the pistol to hide. Pittman testified that instead she gave the pistol to the prison authorities. Pittman said Weaver also gave her some letters to smuggle out of prison.

Pittman testified Weaver told her the trip to Rolla had been to obtain the details of the fort there. She had located the officers' quarters and counted the number of troops. According to Pittman, all of this information was on papers hidden at Mrs. Lingo's house.

Pittman said Weaver had told her that Tilley was on secret business for the Confederacy. However, she said Tilley had not told her what he was after. According to Pittman, Weaver said she had been warned against the detectives, but felt if they were already watching the house it would be hard to escape.

Miss Pittman testified that she, herself, had also been a spy and a smuggler. Pittman said she thought she had met Weaver once before at Confederate GEN Forrest's headquarters. According to Pittman, Weaver brought dispatches from Confederate GEN J. S. Marmaduke to GEN Forrest.

Under cross-examination by Miss Weaver's attorney, Pittman admitted she had spied for Confederate GENs Forrest and Polk. She said she was captured near Fort Pillow, Tennessee, while smuggling guns to Forrest's men.

Miss Pittman testified she had changed her views on the war and now felt the South was wrong. She said she had not taken an oath of allegiance but would be willing to do so. Miss Pittman said she was not positive Weaver was the same lady she talked to in GEN Forrest's headquarters. She also said she had not been put in the prison to act as a federal spy.

Pittman said Weaver had offered her a bribe not to testify. Pittman said Weaver told her GEN Shelby had visited the Weaver home in Batesville the night before she left for St. Louis. Under cross examination, Miss Pittman insisted Weaver revealed most of her story the first night she was in prison.

In the last stage of her testimony, Pittman made it known that when she worked for the South, she put every effort into her job. She also said now that her views had changed, she would work equally hard for the federal cause. Pittman said she advised the prison authorities about Weaver's statements for this reason.

Several other witnesses were then called to testify about locations within the city of St. Louis. The warden of the prison told about the prison routine. One young federal lieutenant told of meeting Miss Weaver while stationed at Batesville.

The next witness was LT Dodge. He testified about receiving the message from Miss Pittman. He spoke of recovering the cut up glove parts from the fireplace. He identified the gloves.

Mrs. E. A. King was recalled to the stand. The Judge Advocate questioned her about the Confederate travel pass she gave to Tilley. Mrs. King admitted giving Tilley a note, but denied knowing it was a pass. She said her aunt gave it to her with instructions to give it to Tilley. She said Tilley put the pass in his pocket and said nothing. She identified her aunt as Mrs. Mitchell of Batesville, Arkansas.

The travel pass read as follows:
Headquarters May 29, 64
Batesville Ark.
All pickets and scouts,

> *Will permit the bearer, W. L. Tilley, two young ladies and one young man, to pass through the Confederate lines and will permit the same, or part, to return again.*
> *By order of*
> *W. B. Woods*
> *Maj. Comdg. Recruits, CSA*

Next to testify were several federal officers who had met Miss Weaver during the occupation of Batesville. All expressed doubt a spy in Batesville could have passed through the federal picket lines. All of these men expressed doubt Weaver was a spy. MAJ William McClellan told the Commission he had placed the slogan, "Col. E. W. Weaver CSA" on Miss Weaver's gloves. The Major said this was done as a joke. McClellan said he had received notes from Miss Weaver. He said on some of these notes she had signed her name as "Col. Weaver."

The prosecution rested its case. The defense then presented a number of witnesses who testified Miss Weaver was a seventeen-year-old child who had traveled frequently in the war-torn country. Most of the witnesses said she had friends among the officer corps of both armies. All of the witnesses said it would be impossible for her to have been a Confederate spy. The defense rested.

The legal representatives for both sides then made lengthy final arguments. In brief, both stressed the high points of their case. Each side pointed out the weak testimony of the opposition. Both sides told the Commission they had proven their side of the controversy beyond doubt.

The Commission agreed with Union Judge Advocate T. A. Post. Miss Weaver was sentenced to be hanged by the neck until dead. The Commission noted two-thirds of its members agreed in the finding.

The case was then referred to the Commanding General of the Department of Missouri for review. GEN W. S. Rosecrans' written remarks concerning the case were brief.

GEN Rosecrans wrote:

> *Proceeding disapproved. The evidence of the guilt of the accused is not sufficiently conclusive. The prisoner will be*

J. B. King

released from custody under the direction of the Provost Marshal General.

Chapter Fourteen

Aftermath

The end of the Civil War brought the people of Missouri back together. In Pulaski County, men from both sides found themselves in a new role as neighbors. In most cases they were able to change from foes to friends without undue difficulty.

Historians are fond of saying that the American Civil War divided the country in a drastic fashion. Instances of brother against brother or father versus son were quite common as men decided for North or South. The division of families went to the very top of society. You may recall that President Lincoln had a Confederate General for a brother-in-law. The people of Pulaski County were also sharply divided by the war.

The last chapter of this book is devoted to gathering up loose ends. You will read about the post-war activity of many people mentioned in the book. You will find bits of history that would not fit in elsewhere. The reader will obtain a new look at some well-established Pulaski County legends. You might even change your views about some of these legends.

At the end of the war, Elizabeth Tilley continued to operate the family farm. One of the first documented acts of the family was to file the will of Wilson M. Tilley, on November 28, 1865. The will was later "proved" on February 14, 1873. This will provides one last glimpse at the Tilley family history.

The heirs of Wilson M. Tilley were recorded as: Mary Ann Morgan, Nancy J. Pippin, Robert L. Christison, Margaret E. Hobbs, Wilson L. Tilley, Mahala L. Collier, and Missaniah Bradford. The witnesses listed on the will were J. A. Rayl, Robert Hudgens, V. B. Hill, and W.W. McDonald.

THE GRAVE MARKER OF ELIZABETH TILLEY. BORN DECEMBER 13, 1807, DIED JANUARY 4, 1892. THE MARKER HAS FALLEN FROM ITS BASE. PHOTOGRAPH BY AUTHOR

This will presents a clear example of the division created in Pulaski County by the war. One witness, V. B. Hill, commanded the first Confederate militia company formed in Pulaski County. In contrast,

J. B. King

J. A. Rayl and W.W. McDonald both served in a Union Army unit, the Forty-eighth Regiment, Missouri Volunteer Infantry. However, prior to the war, Wilson Tilley thought highly enough of these men to ask them to witness his will.

The true story runs deeper upon closer examination. In the 1860 census, J. A. Rayl had a nineteen-year-old store clerk living with his family.

The clerk was Leroy Tilley. In the 1850 census, Vandiver T. Christison lived with Wilson Tilley, but in the 1860 census he lived with V. B. Hill. From these facts, it seems obvious that the families shared a close friendship prior to the war. Yet, the division between North and South split apart these close friends and forced them to become enemies.

On May 1, 1865, Wilson Leroy Tilley was released from the Union military prison at Alton, Illinois. He returned to the family farm. He married, and raised a family.

In the words of Joseph Newkirk Morgan:

Lee Tilley was my grandma's brother. He farmed after the war, and later sold the farm to Uncle William Bradford. He also sold forty acres to my dad. We still refer to it as 'the Tilley field.'

I remember Lee Tilley well, for he used to come by to visit his sister, Mary Ann, who was my grandmother. Lee Tilley was a tall man, and in his old age he used to be able to jump straight up in the air and hit his heels together three times before he hit the floor. Us kids tried to do that, and we could not do it.

After he sold the land, Lee Tilley moved to Columbia, Missouri, where his son, Bruce "Doc" Tilley, went to medical school. After Bruce graduated, the family moved to Plato, Missouri, and Bruce set up a medical practice there.

Another member of the Tilley family who made his mark in Pulaski County after the war was William Bradford. At the age of twenty-two, he enlisted in the Missouri State Guard for six months. When this term expired, he enlisted in the First Missouri Cavalry. His

Civil War battle record was extensive. He was in many battles, including Pea Ridge, Iuka, Corinth, Grand Gulf, Baker's Creek, Big Black, and the siege at Vicksburg. He was captured when Vicksburg fell.

He was paroled by the Union Army and rejoined his unit. He fought in a second series of battles which included Kennesaw Mountain, Jonesboro, Dalton, Altoon Mountain, Franklin, and was captured a second time when Ft. Blakely fell. This time he was held in a prisoner of war camp until the war was over.

THE GRAVE OF WILLIAM L. BRADFORD AND HIS WIFE MISSANIAH SOPHIA (TILLEY) BRADFORD. THE GRAVE IS LOCATED IN THE BRADFORD CEMETERY. PHOTOGRAPH BY AUTHOR.

Bradford returned to Pulaski County in 1866. One of the first people he met was Missaniah S. Tilley. According to page ninety-one of the Methodist Church history, they were married on January 6, 1867. If you read page ninety-two of the same book, you will notice they were married October 26, 1862. It is unknown which is correct.

Following his army career, Bradford became a full-time farmer and entered Pulaski County politics. Beginning in 1882, he was elected once as sheriff, twice as county collector, once as a county court judge, and once as county representative. Although Bradford was reportedly wounded thirteen times during the Civil War, he died at age ninety-five, on July 21, 1934. He was buried in the Bradford Cemetery on Route H, a short distance south of Interstate 44.

THE BRADFORD CEMETERY ON STATE ROAD H NEAR WAYNESVILLE, MISSOURI. PHOTOGRAPH BY AUTHOR.

Another man who settled in Pulaski County after the war was William C. Kerr. The aftermath of the prisoner killing evidently left Kerr a marked man in the army. He was dismissed from the army on January 1, 1864, by Special Order No. 1 from the Missouri Adjutant General. This order was not located in the archives' files, so the actual reason for his dismissal remains unknown.

Kerr settled in Cullen Township near the Roubidoux Creek. His close neighbor across the creek was Wilson L. Tilley. Kerr was elected surveyor of Pulaski County on April 11, 1866. That same year, he purchased eighty acres of U.S. government land located in Section 31, Township 36, Range 11. On this land, he built and operated Kerr's Mill for many years.

In 1872, the Pulaski County Circuit Court condemned the Pulaski County Courthouse. The state of Missouri appropriated two thousand dollars to help build a new courthouse. William C. Kerr was named Superintendent of Construction. He was told to erect a building sixty feet long by forty feet wide and twenty-two feet high. The walls were to be of brick. The total cost of the project was to be between eight- and nine-thousand dollars. This building stood until destroyed by fire in 1903.

William C. Kerr died in 1915, and was buried in the Bradford Cemetery on Route H. His grave was close to the spot where another of his neighbors, William Bradford would later be laid to rest.

THE RESTING PLACE OF LT. WILLIAM C. KERR, FIFTH REGIMENT OF CAVALRY, MISSOURI STATE MILITIA. KERR WAS BORN IN CANADA IN 1839 AND DIED IN PULASKI COUNTY, MISSOURI, IN 1915. PHOTOGRAPH BY AUTHOR

Throughout this book, various members of the Lingo family of Pulaski County have been mentioned. At the start of the war, Dr. Lingo had a drugstore on the Waynesville square. On September 12, 1863, a Union Army patrol near Houston, Missouri killed William Lingo, along with two other Pulaski County men.

In the trial of Miss Emily Weaver, Mrs. Mary Jane Lingo gave testimony. Later in the trial, her daughter, Laura Belle Lingo testified.

J. B. King

The ladies made it known they were ex-Pulaski County residents. Mrs. Lingo made a statement that Laura Belle and Wilson L. Tilley had known each other for many years, since the families had lived close together near Waynesville.

In nearly every account of the Lingo family, the last name has been spelled Lingo. Unfortunately, the census of 1860 does not list a single Lingo. However, the census of 1860 does list a B. G. Lenigow, age forty, who was a physician. His wife, Mary J. was also forty years old. His son, William H. was age nineteen, and his daughter, Laura Belle was seventeen years old.

Which set of records should be believed?

The census enumerator of Pulaski County in 1860 was a local resident, U.S. Marshal John B. Ellis. With his background in law enforcement work and the special care given to census records, it appears Lenigow would be correct. It does seem easy to assume that anyone who heard the name Lenigow pronounced, could well write it down as Lingo. In the study of history, names, dates, and places frequently differ from source to source. It is unclear which name is correct.

Another example of a divided Pulaski County can be found in the brief mention given to the name Lemons. The census of 1860 lists seven families with a last name of Lemons, all living in the Big Piney-Heath Hollow area. In addition, three families with the last name spelled Lemon were also recorded in the southeast corner of Pulaski County, near Big Piney.

All of these families have the oldest members of the household listed with a Southern birthplace. The state of Kentucky was listed for most of them. With a common birthplace, living in the same small section of the county, and a last name almost alike, it seems reasonable to believe they might have been related.

During the investigation into the killing of the prisoners by LT Kerr, the Lemons name was mentioned. LT Francis Reichert, Thirteenth MSM, told about the shooting of James and Washington Lemons. One Lemons was killed and the other wounded. Reichert did not specify which Lemons was killed.

The Tilley Treasure

In July of 1865, the Union militia company, formed in Pulaski County, listed a Willis B. Lemons, age thirty-nine, of Herd Hollow. A second man listed was Charles W. Lemons, age twenty-two, of Smith Hollow. With some Lemons in the Union Army, and others being shot by the Union Army, it appears the Civil War was a bitter time for the Lemons' family.

Another case of guess-the-correct-name concerns a man named Dodds. On September 12, 1863, William Lingo, Obe Moss, and Jacob Bottom from Pulaski County were killed by federal troops near Houston, Missouri. Just before the shooting started, a man identified as Martin Dodds left the group of bushwhackers and went to a nearby town.

The census of 1860 does not list a Martin Dodds, but does have a Milton C. Dodds, age forty-two, from Tennessee. Later, in July of 1865, Milton C. Dodds, age forty-seven, from Gasconade River, appears on the muster roll of Union Army men from Waynesville. Is this the same man? Did he switch sides?

Major John B. Kaiser, Fifth MSM, sent a scout toward Big Piney, Missouri, in December of 1864. The members of this detail found three deserters from Company C, Forty-eighth Missouri Infantry (Union), hiding in a cave near Big Piney. The Union troops killed all three of the hiding men. The dead men were identified as I. S. Williams, Lewis Williams, and Levi Clark. The Union Army report stated a confederate pass was found on the body of I. S. Williams.

The records of Company C, Forty-eighth Missouri Infantry, show Levi Clark deserted his post at Rolla on November 21, 1864. Lewis Williams and I. S. Williams are not mentioned. It appears Levi Clark may have recovered from his fatal wounds, for he filed a will in Pulaski County Probate Court on August 21, 1871. Then again, maybe the Union Army men got the wrong name. It is unknown who was killed by the patrol.

If you were curious about the fate of Miss Emily Weaver, here's a final word on her. Following her release from the military prison

J. B. King

she returned to Batesville, Arkansas. On December 20, 1866, she married Isaac N. Reed. It appears the couple lived happily ever after.

In a large number of books and documents, a well-known Pulaski County Civil War figure was named Hugh McCain. In gathering research material for this book, a copy of a report issued by the Pulaski County Board of Assessment in 1862 was obtained. This man was a member of the board and signed his name as Hugh McCoin. However, his name frequently appears as Hugh McCain on other documents.

In previously published accounts of Pulaski County history, the story of the nine hundred Union troops who seized Waynesville in June of 1862 has received a lot of publicity. The march of twelve thousand Union men through Pulaski County in January of 1862 has received very little attention. The twelve thousand men who marched through here eventually ended their trip at the Battle of Pea Ridge, Arkansas.

It seems hard to believe their trip through Pulaski and Laclede Counties could be forgotten when you recall they ran out of food between Waynesville and Lebanon. Imagine a cold and desolate January with twelve thousand hungry federal locusts swarming over the countryside in search of food. Every corn crib, root cellar, and hog lot must have had its own private squad of soldiers busy loading it up and carting it away. When you add the forage required for the horses and mules that accompanied the twelve thousand troops, one wonders how the local people survived the winter.

As a rule, the troops did not exactly live up to the old Ozark expression of eating "high on the hog." One of the quotes that was not used in the book came from the Rolla Bandmaster, Charles Monroe Chase.

In 1861, he wrote:

We had boiled potatoes, fried pork, and hard crackers for breakfast this morning. The potatoes were quite a treat.

Besides the hardship brought to the local people by the seizure of food, the events of war created other hazards. In the book there is an account of a group of Confederate prisoners marching through the county in December of 1862. The prisoner in charge of the medical issues for these Confederates was Henry Martyn Cheavens. As the captured men marched through Pulaski County, Cheavens suspected some of them suffered from smallpox. In 1862, smallpox was greatly feared for it caused a large number of deaths each year.

In relating the account of the march of the twelve thousand federal troops through Pulaski County, an obscure federal officer, Captain Philip Sheridan, was quoted. Although the Civil War saw him become a famous Union General, his post-war military action against various American Indian tribes brought even greater fame. Starting with his appointment in 1868 as commander of the greatly expanded Department of Missouri, he was involved in the Indian wars for many years.

During his career his troops fought Cheyenne, Sioux, Arapaho, Kiowa, and Comanche Indians. Although he usually won his campaigns, one of his subordinate commanders was General George A. Custer. Custer and his Seventh U.S. Cavalry died on June 25, 1876, in the most infamous cavalry defeat of the Indian wars. When you consider the nationally-known events of American history in which Sheridan was involved, it seems hard to believe that once upon a time he searched desperately for food in Pulaski County.

Another famous general who was mentioned in this book was Grenville Mellan Dodge. You may recall he first appeared as commander of the Fourth Iowa Infantry at Rolla. He ordered Union troops into Dent County for a series of small battles with Confederate COL Freeman. A fact not mentioned in this book concerns Dodge's role in the trial of W. L. Tilley. General Dodge issued Special Order No. 16 on January 16, 1865. This order appointed the military commission which tried W. L. Tilley.

After the war, Grenville Dodge joined the Union Pacific Railroad as its Chief Engineer. For well over a decade, he was one of the most famous railroad men in U.S. history. During this time he helped build over nine-thousand miles of rail lines, as the American frontier moved West.

Another Union General from this book was Franz Sigel. He first appeared in Waynesville in early 1861, leading his men to Springfield. After the defeat at Wilson's Creek, he retreated through Pulaski County to Rolla. He commanded the Rolla post for a brief time and then transferred to the Army of the Potomac. His military career was quite stormy. He resigned from the army in 1865, and moved to New York City.

Union General Samuel Ryan Curtis appeared several times in the book. He was appointed to command the Department of Missouri on several occasions and was removed each time. He died on December 26, 1866, eight months after his discharge from the army.

Confederate General John Sappington Marmaduke also had a good post-war record. When last mentioned in this book, Marmaduke had just been captured by Union troops at Mine Creek, Kansas, on October 25, 1864. The capture came near the end of Price's great raid. Due to his impressive record as a commander, the Union Army refused to parole him. He was sent to a prison camp near Boston, Massachusetts.

In August of 1865, he was released from prison. He later returned to Missouri and became active in politics. His Confederate record did not prove to be a handicap, for he was elected governor of Missouri in 1884. He died while serving in that office on December 28, 1887.

In the book it was noted several times that both of Missouri's wartime civil governments issued money to help run the state. After the war the question of how to redeem this money created severe political problems. The question was resolved after a long struggle in 1875. Missourians adopted a new state constitution which contained a specific provision that all of Missouri's Civil War claims were declared to be null and void. The wartime money became worthless.

One of the most impressive reminders of the Civil War in Pulaski County still stands. The old stagecoach stop on the Waynesville square was reportedly commandeered by the Union Army in 1862. The building then served as a regimental hospital until the end of the war.

When it was first established in 1862, the man in charge was Doctor John Fetzer, a surgeon in the Thirteenth MSM. Dr. Fetzer joined the Union Army on March 14, 1862. He listed his home as

Boonville, Missouri. He remained in charge of the hospital until he resigned from the army on July 25, 1864.

Dr. Fetzer had two assistant surgeons under his command. The first one was Dr. Alexander Fekete who was from Boonville. Dr. Fekete joined the army on March 19, 1862, and was mustered out at the expiration of his service term on April 13, 1865. The second doctor was J. H. Williams, also of Boonville. He joined July 9, 1863, and mustered out April 3, 1865. Details of the stagecoach stop as a Civil War hospital are scarce.

THE OLD STAGECOACH STOP IN WAYNESVILLE. THE BUILDING WAS TAKEN OVER BY THE UNION ARMY IN JUNE OF 1862 AND SERVED AS A HOSPITAL DURING THE CIVIL WAR. PHOTOGRAPH BY AUTHOR.

If you live in Dixon, Crocker, or Richland, Missouri, and were curious why your town was not mentioned in the book, there is a simple answer. Your town did not exist during the Civil War. The founding of these towns in our county history was linked to the progress of the railroad lines across Pulaski County. The present day rail lines were not constructed until the Civil War was over.

This doesn't mean there was an absence of railroad activity in Pulaski County before the war. In fact, there was a fairly large-scale effort to build a rail line across the county prior to the Civil War. If you know where to look today, you can find a series of rail "cuts" across several hills in the county. The proposed line ran east to west just south of the present-day Interstate 44. At one point, construction of a rail tunnel near the Ft. Wood Spur had begun. The west end of this project was located near the Roubidoux Creek on Ft. Wood. The construction efforts are still visible today.

The Census of 1860 listed a large number of Irish and German railroad laborers living in Pulaski County at the start of the war. The census also lists several civil engineers for the rail line who lived near Waynesville. All efforts to build the rail line died early in the war.

During the post-war period in Pulaski County, the old line was abandoned. A new route was surveyed across the northern part of Pulaski County. It may be that the new rail line followed the so called "high road" that was used by Union Army supply wagons. In any event, the new rail line helped create the towns of Dixon, Crocker, and Richland.

During the post-war period, a number of men from the Fifth Regiment of Cavalry, Missouri State Militia, who had served here in the war, made Pulaski County their new home. Settling in Tavern Township was Sergeant William F. Burks of Company H. He was joined by Corporal John A. McGowen from Company E. In Cullen Township, Private William Sublet of Company E bought three hundred ninety-eight acres of U.S. land. He was joined by Private Green D. Hale of Company F. Lieutenant William C. Kerr of Company B has already been mentioned.

If you are interested in an ancestor who may have served in the Civil War in Pulaski County, you should know that as a part of the 1890 Federal Census, a special survey of Civil War veterans was assembled. The survey runs by county and makes a great starting point for research.

While gathering Civil War material for this book, many odd facts about the war were discovered. It can be safely stated that the American Civil War was marked by many unusual situations. One of the oddest stories found concerned the *United States Ship (USS) Wyoming.*

The *Wyoming*, under Captain David S. McDougal, was looking for an enemy commerce raider, the *Confederate States Ship (CSS) Alabama*. The *USS Wyoming* did not find the *CSS Alabama*. But while searching on July 16, 1863, the *Wyoming* was attacked by a fleet of small vessels. In a short naval battle, the *Wyoming* sunk or damaged several of these ships.

This incident has nothing whatever to do with Pulaski County history. The battle occurred in the Straits of Shimonoseki, near Yokohama, Japan. The attacking vessels were Japanese. Where was the *Alabama*?

Along the same lines, another raider, the *CSS Shenandoah* created a problem for some time after the war ended. The *Shenandoah* was quite busy sinking Yankee fishing vessels, thus depriving the Union Army of fresh fish. The *Shenandoah* was finally located by a British battle cruiser and was told the war was over. The ship made for a British port and surrendered to British authorities. It would probably be safe to assume that the Southern sailors were quite happy to depart from their assigned patrol area of the Arctic Ocean, near the North Pole.

The American Civil War was marked by approximately ten-thousand four hundred fifty-five military actions. These actions ranged from very minor skirmishes to major battles, such as Bull Run. The state recording the most military actions was Virginia with two-thousand, one hundred fifty-four. In second place was Tennessee, with one thousand, four hundred sixty-two. In third place was Missouri with one-thousand, one hundred sixty-two military actions.

In December of 1864, MAJ John B. Kaiser reported he "sent a scout of six men in a northeast direction (from Waynesville), who returned Dec. 2nd and succeeded in killing a bad character by the name of Charles Withers." The census of 1860 lists a Charles Withers, age twenty-four, from Kentucky. Withers was listed as a laborer. His wife was Delilah, age twenty-four, and he had two children, Laura J., age two, and William D., age seven months.

Another landmark in the Civil War action of Pulaski County was a famous inn, the California House. The house was built on land owned by William and Sarah Maxey. The Maxeys bought the land on February 19, 1840, from the St. Louis-San Francisco Railroad. Other records show that on October 30, 1860, Hugh McCain purchased the inn.

The inn was located next to the St. Louis to Springfield Road. It began operating in 1857. During the war, as noted in this book, there were numerous skirmishes fought near the inn. In post-war Pulaski County, the California House was torn down and later rebuilt.

You can still drive by the inn today and get an idea of what it looked like during the Civil War. When the home was rebuilt, the same basic floor plan as the original was followed. Indeed, part of the lumber and timber used during the reconstruction came from the first California House. Today the former inn serves as the home of Emerson and Marie Storie of Laquey.

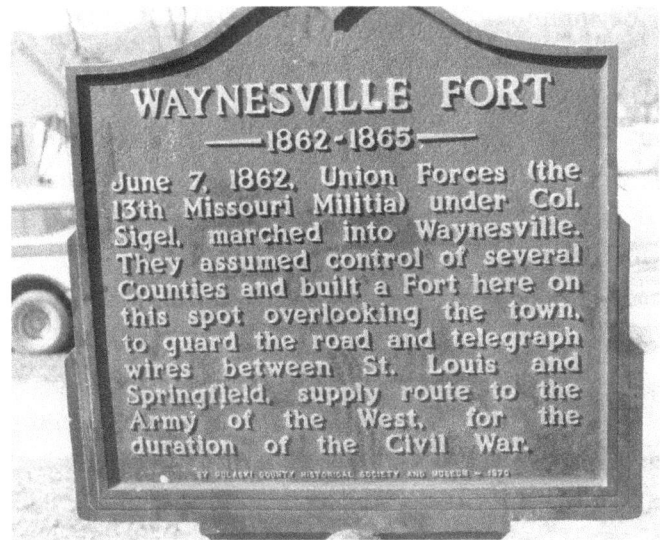

THE SITE OF THE UNION ARMY POST AT WAYNESVILLE, MISSOURI, IS SHOWN BY A HISTORICAL MARKER. THE SIGN IS LOCATED ON FORT STREET JUST SOUTH OF THE WAYNESVILLE CITY SQUARE. PHOTOGRAPH BY AUTHOR.

The Tilley Treasure

Local historians place much faith in a book by Goodspeed Publishing Company of Chicago. The book was first printed in 1889. The book is entitled *History of Laclede, Camden, Dallas, Webster, Wright, Texas, Pulaski, Phelps, and Dent Counties, Missouri.*

During the time the research for Goodspeed's book was underway, all of the Pulaski County Courthouse records were available for study. In addition, people who helped make the history of Pulaski County were still alive and available for interview.

Modern-day research has severe handicaps. The people active in our local history have been gone for many years. The fire which destroyed the Pulaski County Courthouse in 1903 also reduced the majority of the old records to ashes. Research into Pulaski County history before 1903 presents an author with a very hard task. The documents needed for accurate work are very hard to locate.

Thus, the importance of Goodspeed's book in local history cannot be overemphasized. A successful challenge as to the accuracy of Goodspeed's Pulaski County history might well be impossible. In gathering material for this book, information was acquired which might cast some shadow of doubt about Goodspeed's accuracy concerning the capture of Waynesville in 1862.

Quoting from Goodspeed:

On the evening of June 7, 1862 the Federals under Col. Albert Sigel came in on the Rolla road, entering from the east. Some of the citizens had gone to the western bluff overlooking Waynesville, and watched the army, but Col. Sigel sent a cavalry company over and captured them. The soldiers first cut down the rebel flagpole, chopped it up, and threw it in the creek; then they rifled the stores and McCormick's Saloon. They had practiced on a store owned by G. W. Colley, near the California House, then owned by a strong Union man named Hugh McCoin.

In December of 1863, COL Albert Sigel wrote a short historical memorandum addressed to the Adjutant General, State of Missouri. In this report, COL Albert Sigel clearly stated:

J. B. King

Companies A, B, C, and F started from Boonville, June 1, 1862, by way of California, Tuscumbia, to Waynesville, distance one hundred miles, where they arrived June 7, 1862, under command of Col. Albert Sigel.

Colonel Albert Sigel commanded these four companies of the Thirteenth MSM as they moved south from Tuscumbia to Waynesville according to Goodspeed's record:

They had practiced on a store owned by G. W. Colley, near the California House...

However, this was prior to their arrival in town. How did they enter Waynesville from the east? The historical location of the California House in Pulaski County history cannot be challenged. As previously stated, you can drive by it today, seven miles west of Waynesville.

History can be confusing. You may recall the advance of GEN Lyon upon Jefferson City, Missouri, on June 14, 1861. At the same time he advanced on Jefferson City, Lyon ordered COL Franz Sigel to take nine hundred Home Guards and follow the St. Louis to Springfield Road through Pulaski County. COL Franz Sigel's troops were to stop at Springfield. Sigel's advance reached Springfield on June 23, 1861. COL Franz Sigel's men had to enter Waynesville from the east side.

If you would like more confusion, COL Albert Sigel's force of four companies should have numbered approximately eight hundred men. Thus, there were two COL Sigels in Waynesville during June, one year apart almost to the day, with a force of men closely matched in numbers. One Sigel had to enter Waynesville from the east. Did the other Sigel enter town from the west?

In his end of the year report for 1864, LTC Eppstein, Fifth MSM, described the arms of his unit. Eppstein said:

The arms in possession of the regiment are in good condition. About three hundred Smith & Wesson's rifles have been purchased by the men, which is a very effective and desirable cavalry arm.

The reference to the Smith & Wesson's rifles probably caught your eye, if you are familiar with the history of firearms. It appears Eppstein may have been mistaken in his identification of the firearms. Mr. Roy Jinks, the Chief Historian for Smith & Wesson firearms company, doubts Eppstein's accuracy.

Mr. Jinks said, in a letter dated November 21, 1983:

I have done considerable research in the Smith & Wesson records and can find no reference to Smith & Wesson producing a rifle during the Civil War period... It is my honest opinion the company (5th MSM) probably purchased Smith Carbines which were manufactured by Massachusetts Arms Company and The American Machine Works of Springfield, Massachusetts. It is very possible that they could have confused them with our firm.

On the morning of September 12, 1863, Union Captain S. B. Richardson's unit killed three bushwhackers. These men were identified as William Lingo, Obe Moss, and Jacob Bottom. A fourth man was shot through both thighs and captured. You may recall that this man, Oscar D. Blount, gave CPT Richardson a statement concerning the activity of several people, including W. L. Tilley. Unfortunately, the National Archives' staff in Washington, D. C. was unable to locate that written statement.

In his report, CPT Richardson said Oscar D. Blount was from St. Louis, Missouri. CPT Richardson also said he would send the statement and recovered property to the Rolla Headquarters with the next wagon train. A record of a military trial for Oscar D. Blount could not be located at the National Archives.

Since Rolla was the Headquarters of the unit, it appears quite probable Oscar D. Blount was sent to Rolla. On October 21, 1863, the Union Army at Rolla mustered in a new recruit. His name was Oscar D. Blount. Private Blount was assigned to Company A, Twelfth Regiment, Missouri Cavalry Volunteers. PVT Blount, who listed his home as St. Louis, Missouri, was mustered out of the army on June 27, 1865.

J. B. King

On June 28, 1861, Captain Josiah C. Smith, Fifth MSM, submitted a patrol report in which he described the capture of S. S. Tucker. CPT Smith reported that after he paroled S. S. Tucker, he discovered the man's name was actually Benson Woods. Woods had been with a group of bushwhackers when captured.

During the trial of Wilson Leroy Tilley, witness Howell Bryant of Waynesville also mentioned the name Woods. According to Bryant's testimony, the leader of the bushwhackers who rode with COL Love's men was named Woods. Bryant said Woods was wounded in the skirmish at King's farm. Bryant testified that Tilley then took command of the bushwhackers. Was this the same Woods CPT Smith captured in 1861?

One fact, not mentioned in the book, concerns a private citizen who was with CPT Smith's unit the day Woods was captured. CPT Smith's report said:

And here allow me to mention the noteworthy conduct of William Wilson, a citizen of this place, who evinced true courage and determination in chasing up and capturing these outlaws despite having his horse shot under him, but never faltering as long as anything was to be done.

In the report issued by the Pulaski County Board of Assessment on November 28, 1862, William Wilson was listed as a member of the board. In other records, William Wilson was listed as a member of the Pulaski County Administrative Court. These records show he was elected on July 11, 1864, and again on May 20, 1865.

You may recall that as Lieutenant C. C. Twyford rode toward his capture at King's farm, his mission was to locate a man named Benjamin Moore. The Pulaski County Militia muster roll for July 6, 1865, listed a Benjamin R. Moore, age twenty. On August 7, 1865, Benjamin R. Moore became the sheriff of Pulaski County.

Moore replaced George W. Colley who had become sheriff on May 20, 1865. You may recall that after one of the numerous skirmishes at the California House, Mr. G. W. Colley was detailed to assist with the burial of the dead. In June of 1862, his store near the

California House had been looted by the men of the Thirteenth MSM prior to their arrival in Waynesville. In September of 1864, G. W. Colley joined Company A, Forty-eighth Missouri Infantry.

THE GRAVE OF CYRUS COLLEY. COLLEY WAS ONE OF THE FIRST WHITE MEN TO SETTLE IN PULASKI COUNTY. AT THE START OF THE CIVIL WAR, HE WAS ONE OF THE MOST ACTIVE CONFEDERATES IN WAYNESVILLE. THE GRAVEYARD AND THE AREA AROUND THE CALIFORNIA HOUSE WERE NAMED IN HIS HONOR. THE COLLEY HOLLOW CEMETERY IS LOCATED LESS THAN ONE MILE FROM THE CALIFORNIA HOUSE. PHOTOGRAPH BY AUTHOR

Another Pulaski County man who joined the Southern cause was Lawyer V. B. Hill. In May of 1861, he helped organize one company of Confederate troops from Pulaski County men. Hill was given the rank of Captain, and later led his Pulaski County men into battle. After the war, Hill returned to Pulaski County. He was elected Superintendent of Public Schools on May 20, 1871. In November of 1872, he was elected prosecuting attorney of Pulaski County.

At the Battle of Wilson's Creek near Springfield, Missouri, in August of 1861, General Lyon had less than six thousand men under his command. The men who survived the fight went on to greater

J. B. King

fame during the war. A total of twenty men who fought at Wilson's Creek rose to the rank of General in the Union Army during the war.

The list contains seven Major Generals: Schofield, Stanley, Steele, Sigel, Granger, Osterhaus, and Herron. A total of thirteen more men became Brigadier Generals. This list included Sturgis, Carr, Plummer, Mitchell, Sweeny, Totton, Gilbert, and Clayton.

The Confederate Army had a similar story. The force of twelve-thousand men at Wilson's Creek included seven men who became Generals in the Southern Army. These men were Price, Parsons, Slack, Shelby, Clark, Greene, and Cockrell.

At the start of the Civil War, Governor Claiborne Fox Jackson advised the Confederate President, Jefferson Davis, that Missouri would give the South 100,000 men for battle. The actual figure was around forty-thousand Missouri men who joined the Southern cause. Missouri furnished the Union Army over 100,000 men.

In reading this book, you may have noticed a tendency for small groups of Union troops to defeat larger Southern units. One reason for this was the fact that most Southern units in Missouri were poorly armed. Many Southern soldiers had only a double barrel shotgun for use in battle. In the trial of W. L. Tilley, several of the captured Union men made reference to the "old guns and pistols" carried by COL Love's men.

Another reason the Union troops looked good was due to the written battle reports. In most of the small skirmishes in Missouri, the Union Army reports are recorded. The Rebel units didn't keep many records. It would be a rare military officer who admitted his unit was defeated by a smaller enemy force. In the same light, victory looks better if the enemy force was much bigger. Since the Confederate records are not available, only one side of the picture is represented.

Who killed Wilson M. Tilley? As recounted in the book, a number of accounts concerning his death have been published. You may recall his great grandson, Joseph Newkirk Morgan, put the blame on bushwhackers. You may recall the scare experienced by George Morgan the day after Tilley's death. Morgan's report places drunken outlaws near the crime scene the following day. Since the two locations are less than one mile apart, these bushwhackers make very logical suspects.

When you consider their treatment of young George Morgan, the killing of Wilson M. Tilley for his money becomes quite possible. However, one more fact helps cast the blame on lawless bushwhackers.

In the eyes of the Union Army during 1864, Wilson M. Tilley was a known Confederate sympathizer. Under the wartime conditions, a Union unit could have legally killed him if firearms were found in his possession. A report of such action by a Union unit would not have caused much concern in 1864. The guerrilla war in Missouri was repeatedly marked by cases of injustice against Missouri citizens by the Union Army. These cases are documented in official records submitted by the Union officers who ordered these acts.

As an example, consider the "Palmyra Massacre" on October 18, 1862. During one of his raids into north Missouri, Confederate Colonel Porter moved through Palmyra, Missouri. His men kidnapped a man named Andrew Allsman, a noted Union man.

Shortly after the raid on Palmyra, all of the men taken from the town were released by Porter. Allsman was not released, and was never heard from again. It was rumored Porter's men had executed him.

Union General John McNeil issued a public order to COL Porter to release Allsman within ten days. McNeil's order stated that failure to comply would result in the execution of ten Confederate sympathizers. Allsman did not appear. On October 18, 1862, General McNeil's troops executed ten men chosen at random.

The records kept by the Union Army report the Palmyra Massacre in detail, including the names of the ten men who were executed. No such reports have been found for Wilson M. Tilley in the Union Army files.

In the end, one question remains: Who killed Wilson M. Tilley?

J. B. King

One last look at the coins of Wilson M. Tilley. His story and his coins are now part of Ozark folklore. Photograph by Author

Bibliography

Adamson, Hans C., *Rebellion in Missouri 1861. Nathaniel Lyon and His Army of the West*. 1961.

Archives, Missouri National Guard. Jefferson City, Missouri.

Beers, Henry Putney., *Guide to the Archives of the Government of the Confederate States of America*.

Brownies, R. S., *Gray Ghosts of the Confederacy Guerrilla Warfare in the West 1860-1865*, 1958.

Catton, Bruce., *The Civil War*, 1980.

Crowley, William J., *Tennessee Cavalier in the Missouri Cavalry*, 1978.

Easley, Virginia., *Journal of the Civil War in Missouri 1861, Henry Martyn Cheavens*, October 1961. Missouri Historical Review, 56.

Encyclopedia Britannica.

Fort Gateway Daily Guide.

Grant, Ulysses S., *Personal Memoirs*, 2 volumes. 1885-1886.

History of Laclede, Camden, Dallas, Webster, Wright, Texas, Pulaski, Phelps, and Dent County Missouri. Chicago: Goodspeed Publishing Company. 1889.

Library of Congress, Photo Duplication Service.

Long, E. B., and Barbara Long., *The Civil War Day by Day: An Almanac 1861-1865*. 1971.

Knox, Thomas W., *Campfire and Cotton Field: Southern Adventure in Time of War,* 1865.

Moss, James E., *Missouri Confederate in the Civil War: The Journal of Henry Martyn Cheavens 1862-1863*, Missouri Historical Review, 57.

Mottaz, Mabel M., *Lest We Forget*.

Munden, Kenneth, and Henry Putney Beers., *Guide to the Federal Archives Relating to the Civil War*.

Monaghan, Jay., *Civil War on the Western Border 1854-1865*, 1955.

Monaghan, Jay, Editor-in-Chief., *The Book of the American West*, 1963.

National Archives. Washington D.C. Record Group 393, #460, #1338, #1339, and #1340.

Old Settlers' Gazette, Volume I.

Parrish, William E., *A History of Missouri*, Volume II and Volume III.

Parrish, William E., T*urbulent Partnership Missouri and the Union 1861-1865*, 1963.

Pulaski County Democrat.

Schofield, John M., *46 Years in the Army,* 1897.

Sheridan, Philip H., *Personal Memoirs*, 2 volumes., 1902.

Sigel, Franz., *Military Operations in Missouri in the Summer and Autumn of 1861,* Missouri Historical Review, 26.

The Pioneer's News.

The Pulaski County Historical Society., History Pulaski County Missouri., 1982.

Trial Transcript. *United States v. Tilley.*

Trial Transcript. *United States v. Weaver.*

Tri-Weekly Missouri Republican.

Turpin, Thomas., *Our Ancestors in Pulaski County,* Volume I and Volume II.

United States Census. 1840, 1850, 1860, and 1890.

War of the Rebellion: Official Records of the Union and Confederate Armies., 4 series, 70 Volumes., Washington D.C.1880-1902.

Welsh, Donald H., *A Union Band Director Views Camp Rolla 1861*, Missouri Historical Review, 55.

Williams, Walter, and Floyd Shoemaker., *Missouri; Mother of the West.*, Volume II, 1930.

Wolff, Theodore H., *A History of the Methodist Society at Waynesville, Missouri 1838 to 1963.*

INDEX

A

Acock, A.: 66

Adams, R. and Son: 57, 67

Alabama, CSS: 206

Alexander, J.: 67

Allen, Dan: 66

Allsman, Andrew: 216

Altoon Mountain: 196

Anderson, Bloody Bill: 114, 115

Anderson, Robert, MAJ, USA: 12

Anthony: 118

Arapaho Indians: 202

Arkansas, Arkadelphia: 84

Arkansas, Batesville: 62, 63, 67, 75, 79, 119, 131, 147-152, 154, 155, 160, 163, 176, 180, 182, 185-187, 189, 190, 201

Arkansas, Crane Hill: 113

Arkansas, Johnson County: 85

Arkansas, Little Rock: 61, 63, 64, 72, 75, 180, 181, 186

Arkansas, Pea Ridge: 36, 37, 196, 201

Avey, Francis M., LT, USA: 53, 161

B

Baldwin, John Y., SGT, USA: 121

Barstow, W. A., COL, USA: 131, 146

Bartle and Son: 66

Bartlett, Soloman, 2LT, USA: 166, 171

Bates, Uriah, LT, USA: 95, 96, 98,99, 104, 109, 118

Baushausen, Julius H., LT, USA: 96-106, 108

Bell, J. Warren: 165

Bench, E. D.: 67

Bench, J.: 67

Benton, Thomas Hart: 19

Benz, August, CPT, USA: 119

Berry, S.: 66

Beveridge, COL, USA: 111, 112

Big Black: 196

Big Piney: 43, 44, 101, 109, 115, 117, 118, 121, 128, 199, 200

Black, Thomas G., CPT, USA: 45

Black, William: 66

Black's: 115

Blair, F.: 66

Blair, Frank, GEN, USA: 14-16, 19, 71

Blakey, G. B., PVT, CSA: 53, 55, 58, 61

Blount, Oscar D.: 83, 210

Bonaparte, Napoleon: 34

Booth, John Wilkes: 122

Boston Mountains: 36

Bottom, Jacob: 83, 200, 210

Bowen, MAJ, USA: 30, 31

Box, R.: 67

Bradford (Tilley), Missaniah Sophia: 5, 193-196

Bradford, William L.: 22, 43, 195-198

Bray, Daniel: 66

Bristoe, CPT, USA: 90, 140

Brown, H. B., LT, USA: 53, 55, 58-60

Brown, R.: 66

Brown, Thomas: 66

Bryant, Howell: 142, 166-172, 211

Bryant, J.: 67

Bulkley, L., CPT, USA: 132

Burkhart: 114

Burks, William F., SGT, USA: 205

Burnett, J. S.: 66

Burr, Edwin: 147, 161, 164, 176-178

Burr, Emma: 177, 178

C

California House: 41, 49, 50, 55, 60, 61, 64, 79, 82, 207-212

Calvert, CPL, USA: 109

Cameron, Simon: 13

Campbell, J., 67

Campbell, J. C., Wright County Justice of Peace: 37, 38, 117

Canada, country of: 60, 198

Candy, John W.: 29

Cantrell, D. W., LT, USA: 115

Carr, Eugene A., BG, USA: 213

Carrill, H. Owen, LT, USA: 97, 99, 102, 105

Carson, James: 39

Carson, S.: 66

Casey, (robber): 81

Chase, Charles Monroe: 20, 22, 201

Cheavens, Henry Martyn: 72, 202, 217, 218

Cheyenne Indians: 202

Christer, Peter, PVT, USA: 96

Christison, Robert L.: 193

Christison, Vandiver T.: 5, 195

Clark, GEN, CSA: 213

Clark, Levi: 117, 206

Clawson, SGT, USA: 118

Clayton, BG, USA: 213

Cockrell, GEN, CSA: 213

Colby, C.: 66

Colby, George: 66

Coleman, W. O., COL, CSA: 43-45, 58, 62

Colley Hollow Cemetery: 65, 212

Colley, Cyrus: 212

Colley, George W.: 65, 208, 209, 211, 212

Collier, David, Dr.: 170, 187

Collier (Tilley), Mahala L.: 5, 187, 193

Comanche Indians: 202

Copeland, Mr.: 84

Cornwell, James (attorney): 132, 156

Craig, Tom, CPT, CSA: 34

Cullen Township: 197, 205

Curtis, Samuel Ryan, MG, USA: 34-36, 47, 63, 64, 78, 94, 113, 162, 203

Custer, George A., GEN, USA: 202

D

David, Rev.: 66

Davis, LTC, Provost Marshall: 165

Davis, Jefferson, President, CSA: 10, 31, 213

Dodds, Martin: 83, 200

Dodds, Milton C.: 200

Dodge, Grenville M., COL/GEN., USA: 29, 30, 202

Dodge, LT, USA: 188, 189

Dutch Hollow/Monday Hollow: 28

E

Eaton, MAJ, USA: 157, 158

Ellis, Byron: 127

Ellis, John B., U. S. Marshall: 199

Eppstein, Joseph A., LTC, USA: 38, 43, 49, 53, 55, 67, 68, 72, 77, 112, 117, 209, 210

Estas, LT, USA: 70

Ewing, Thomas, GEN, USA: 110, 111

F

Fekete, Alexander Dr., USA: 96, 100, 204

Fetzer, John Dr., USA: 203, 204

Fischer, Waldemar, MAJ: 82, 87, 95-99

Freeman, COL, CSA: 29-31, 65, 84, 119, 202

Frémont, John C., MG, USA: 19, 20, 23, 25, 27, 28, 33, 71

Frost, Daniel M., BG, CSA: 13-15

Ft. Blakely: 196

Ft. Sumter: 10-12

G

Gallup, H. A., MAJ, USA: 51-53, 55, 56, 58-60

Gamble, Hamilton R., (attorney) Missouri Gov.: 11, 19, 20, 23, 25, 27, 33, 38, 45 94

Gano, Richard M., GEN, CSA: 130

Gasconade River: 17, 20, 49, 51, 80, 81, 96-99, 100, 103, 104, 200

George, CPL, USA: 59

Gibbs, G.: 66

Gilbert, BG, USA: 213

Glover, John M., COL, USA: 44, 51, 52, 64, 66-68

Goodman, William: 66

Granger, Gordon, MG, USA: 213

Grant, Ulysses S., Gen. USA: 15, 122, 217

Gray, F. O.: 38

Gray, H. Decker: 66

Green, O. D., USA: 106

Greene, Gen., CSA: 213

Griesback, Martin, LT, USA: 96, 97, 101, 119

Grossland, Elijah: 57, 58

Gruesel, COL, USA: 29

H

Hale, Green D., PVT, USA: 205

Hall, Andy: 83

Hall, George H., BG: 131

Hall, Willard P., Missouri Lt. Governor: 19, 94

Halleck, Henry Wager, MG, USA: 33, 34, 41, 42, 64

Hamilton, William: 43

Hamilton, L.: 67

Hammock, William: 66

Hammock, James: 66

Harney, William S., GEN, USA: 14-16

Harris, S.: 66

Heath's Hollow: 57, 199

Heiden, CPT, USA: 37

Helams, Samuel: 66

Helm, Ben Hardin, BG, CSA: 84

Herd Hollow: 200

Herrick, T. P., COL, USA: 132

Herron, Frank J., MG, USA: 79, 213

Hibbs, E.: 66

Hickman, SGT, USA: 118

Hill, V. B., (attorney), CPT, CSA: 15, 194, 195, 212

Hillerich, Adam, LT, USA: 112

Hindman, Thomas C., GEN, CSA: 39, 63, 64

Hirsch, Samuel: 153

Hobbs, Lee: 127

Hobbs (Tilley), Margaret E.: 5, 127, 193

Hoffman, George: 121

Hudgens, Robert: 194

Huff, William: 67

Hunt, GEN, USA: 100

Hunter, David, MG, USA: 28, 33

I

Illinois, Alton: 183, 195

J

Jackson, Claiborne Fox, Missouri Gov.: 9, 10, 12-19, 25-27, 33, 72, 77, 213

Jinks, Roy: 210

Johnson, CPT, CSA: 49

Johnson, Hiram: 66

Johnson's Mill: 43, 109

Judd, William H., CPT, USA: 132

K

Kaiser, John B., MAJ, USA: 107-109, 117, 119, 200, 206

Kansas: 64, 94, 110, 113, 114

Kansas, Ft. Scott: 64, 114

Kansas, Marais des Cygnes: 113, 114

Kansas, Mine Creek: 113, 203

Kennesaw Mountain: 196

Kerr, William C., LT, USA: 51-58, 60, 197-199, 205

Kerry, CPT, CSA: 57

Keyser, Clark, 1LT, USA: 105, 107

Kimmel, William: 66

King, Eleanor A.: 186, 189

King, Hiram: 87-89, 93, 141

King, John: 83

King's Farm: 87-89, 93, 141, 211

Kiowa Indians: 202

Kirby, LT, USA: 29

Knapp, J.: 67

Knetser, Calvin: 66

Knight, G. R. (Dick), Sgt., MSHP: 4

Knox, Thomas W.: 28, 217

L

Lakeway, Joseph : 66

LaMine Bridge: 84

Lawson, Andrew : 119

Lawther, Robert R., COL, CSA: 45, 49, 51, 56, 61

Lee, Robert E., GEN, CSA: 122

Lemon/Lemons Family: 199

Lemons, Charles W.: 200

Lemons, D. Burnett: 66

Lemons, James: 57, 199

Lemons, Washington: 57, 199

Lemons, Willis B.: 200

Lenigow, B. G. Dr., (aka Lingo): 199

Lenigow, Laura B. (aka Lingo): 199

Lenigow, Mary J., (aka Lingo): 199

Lenigow, William H. (aka Lingo): 199

Lewis, Adam: 151, 160, 176

Lewis, S. B., SGT, USA: 119

Lewis, Violet: 176

Lincoln, Abraham; 16th U.S. President: 9, 11, 13, 14, 16, 19, 25, 46, 47, 77, 84, 122, 131, 181, 193

Lincoln, Tad: 11

Lincoln, Willy: 11

Lingo - See Lenigow

Missouri, Linn Creek: 28, 85

Livingston, COL, USA: 147-149, 176, 177

Logan, A: 67

Logan, George: 43, 67

Loney, PVT, USA: 97

Long, CPT, USA: 45, 50

Louisiana, Shreveport: 78

Lounan, Thomas: 66

Love, COL, CSA: 90, 91, 135-143, 174, 175, 211, 213

Lowder, William : 67

Ludlow, CPT: 37

Lusby, A.: 67

Lyon, Nathaniel, GEN, USA: 15-18, 20-22, 26, 71, 209, 212, 217

M

Mace, J. W. "Jap": 2, 4

Mark Twain National Forest: 2

Marmaduke, John Sappington, GEN, CSA: 75-77, 79, 111, 188, 203

Mason, Frank: 90

Maus, Charles B., CPT, USA: 95-100, 104, 105, 107, 109, 117

Maxey, John: 128

Maxey, Sarah: 207

Maxey, William: 207

Maysfield, Fountain, 1LT, CSA: 29

McAfee, John: 10

McCain (McCoin), Hugh : 39, 41, 66, 69, 82, 201, 207, 208

McCartney, A: 67

McClellan, William, MAJ, USA: 190

McCoin - See McCain

McCourtney: 118

McCulloch, Ben, GEN, CSA: 20, 21, 36

McDonald, W. W.: 59, 194, 195

McEll, C.: 67

McGowen, John A., CPL, USA: 205

McKee, H. M.: 172, 187

McKerk Landing: 50

McNabb, D. M.: 66

McNeil, John., GEN, USA: 111, 112, 214

Meadows, John M., PVT, CSA: 53, 55, 58, 61

Meredith, S. A., BG, USA: 131

Merel, D.: 67

Merrill's Crossing: 85

Mexico, country of: 34, 71

Miller, George : 29

Mississippi, Vicksburg: 196

Missouri, Arrow Rock: 85, 113

Missouri, Big Blue: 114

The Tilley Treasure

Missouri, Bloomfield: 79

Missouri, Boonville: 17, 38, 39, 41, 71, 85, 113, 204, 209

Missouri, Buffalo: 29

Missouri, California: 41, 113, 209

Missouri, Camden County: 208, 217

Missouri, Camp Jackson: 14-16, 152, 176

Missouri, Cape Girardeau: 24, 79

Missouri, Carondelet: 186, 187

Missouri, Carrollton: 113

Missouri, Carthage: 18, 20, 85, 113

Missouri, Cassville: 25, 63

Missouri, Cedar County: 85

Missouri, Cole Camp: 84

Missouri, Cole County: 10

Missouri, Cooper County: 38

Missouri, Crocker: 204, 205

Missouri, Cross Timbers: 85

Missouri, Crow's Station: 43

Missouri, Cuba: 111

Missouri, Dallas County: 29, 208, 217

Missouri, Danville: 113

Missouri, Deer Creek: 85

Missouri, Dent County: 29, 65, 202, 208, 217

Missouri, Dixon: viii, 204, 205, 248

Missouri, Douglas County: 37

Missouri, Dug Ford: 85

Missouri, Fond du Lac: 180

Missouri, Fox Creek: 37

Missouri, Ft. Davidson: 110

Missouri, Ft. Leonard Wood: 1, 2, 128, 205, 247

Missouri, Glasgow: 113

Missouri, Granby: 34

Missouri, Greene County: 9

Missouri, Greenfield: 84

Missouri, Hartville: 37, 75, 76, 122

Missouri, Hickman Mills: 114

Missouri, Houston: 1, 43, 44, 77, 79, 82, 98, 109, 119, 198, 200

Missouri, Howard County: 38

Missouri, Howell County: 45

Missouri, Humansville: 84, 85

Missouri, Iberia: 45

Missouri, Independence: 113, 114

Missouri, Ironton,: 24, 110

The Tilley Treasure

Missouri, Jefferson City: 1, 10, 16, 17, 19, 24, 26, 50, 51, 110, 112, 113, 209, 217

Missouri, Johnstown: 85

Missouri, Jonesboro (Jonesborough): 85, 196

Missouri, Laclede County: 35, 37, 44, 80, 201, 208, 217

Missouri, Lafayette County: 38, 60

Missouri, Leasburg: 111

Missouri, Lebanon: 21, 25, 28, 34, 36, 37, 49, 63, 81, 82, 90, 91, 106, 108, 201

Missouri, Lexington: 25, 60, 113, 114

Missouri, Licking: 43, 83

Missouri, Marshall: 113

Missouri, Marshfield: 63, 75

Missouri, Miller County: 44

Missouri, Moniteau County: 38

Missouri, Mountain Grove: 37

Missouri, Mountain Store: 44, 140

Missouri, Neosho: 25, 84

Missouri, Newburg: 128

Missouri, Newtonia: 113

Missouri, Osage County: 50

Missouri, Ozark: 75

Missouri, Palmyra: 214

Missouri, Paris: 113

Missouri, Patterson: 79

Missouri, Phelps County: 44, 208, 217

Missouri, Pilot Knob: 111, 112, 186

Missouri, Pineville: 113

Missouri, Plato: 195

Missouri, Potosi: 16

Missouri, Pulaski County: vii, 1-5, 9, 12, 15, 18, 21, 22, 28, 35, 39, 42, 44, 49, 50, 65-67, 75, 79, 83, 90, 93, 95, 109, 114, 117, 118, 122, 123, 142, 171, 173, 186, 187, 193-209, 211, 212, 217-219

Missouri, Richland: 204, 205

Missouri, Richmond: 115

Missouri, Richwoods: 111

Missouri, Ridgely: 113

Missouri, Rolla: 17, 20-24, 29, 33-39, 42, 44, 51, 52, 54, 59, 63, 64, 66-68, 73, 79-83, 96-99, 101-109, 111, 112, 114, 117, 118, 121, 127, 128, 146, 170, 171, 186-188, 200-204, 208, 210, 219

Missouri, Russellville: 113

Missouri, Salem: 30, 45, 84, 117, 119, 186, 247

Missouri, Saline County: 38

Missouri, Sand Springs: 75

Missouri, Scott's Ford: 85

Missouri, Sedalia: 113

Missouri, Shelby County: 10

Missouri, Smithville: 113

Missouri, Springfield: 17

Missouri, St. Clair: 111

Missouri, St. James: 111

Missouri, St. Louis: 1, 11, 13-17, 44, 51, 71, 72, 83, 94, 106, 110-112, 131, 146, 151, 152, 156, 164, 165, 172, 176, 179, 180, 185-189, 207, 209, 210

Missouri, Steelville: 111

Missouri, Stockton: 84

Missouri, Syracuse: 84

Missouri, Texas County: 29, 49, 114, 122

Missouri, Thomasville: 83

Missouri, Tipton: 84

Missouri, Tuscumbia: 41, 209

Missouri, Union: 111

Missouri, Warsaw: 84

Missouri, Washington: 111

Missouri, Washington County: 16

Missouri, Waverly: 113

Missouri, Waynesville: 1, 2, 4, 5, 8, 12, 15, 21, 39, 44-47, 49, 50, 61, 63, 64, 67, 68, 72, 75, 77, 80-85, 87, 90, 91, 95-106, 109, 113-115, 117-119, 121-123, 125-127, 134, 139, 166-168, 171, 182, 198-209, 211, 212

Missouri, Webster County: 208, 217

Missouri, West Plains: 45

Missouri, Westport: 113

Missouri, Wright County: 34, 44, 81, 208, 217

Missouri River: 50, 64, 113

Mitchell, A.: 66

Mitchell, H.: 66

Mitchell, Robert B., BG, USA: 213

Mitchell, Mrs.: 189

Mitchell, Mr.: 171

Monday Hollow/Dutch Hollow: 28

Moore, Benjamin: 87, 211

Morgan (Tilley), Mary Ann: 3, 5, 127, 193, 195

Morgan, George: 127, 213

Morgan, John: 127

Morgan, Joseph Newkirk: viii, 2, 3, 127, 129, 195, 213, 214

Morgan, Reuben: 3

Moss, Obe, LT, CSA: 83, 200, 210

Mudd, Alexis, MAJ, USA: 21

Muller, George, CPT, USA: 82, 96, 97, 102, 105

Muntzell, LT, USA: 70, 109, 117, 122

Murphy, Richard, CPT, USA: 49, 50, 64, 82, 83, 98-106, 122

N

Newberry, MAJ, USA: 117

O

Oak Hill, Battle of: 21

Odle, John C., 121

Ogletree, O.: 66

Oliver, Mordecai; Missouri Secretary of State: 19

Ormsby, James: 43

Orr, Sample: 9

Osage River: 17, 85

Osterhaus, Peter J., MG, USA: 213

P

Pacific Railroad: 17, 20

Palmyra Massacre: 214

Parker, Allen, PVT, USA: 140

Parsons, Monroe M., GEN, CSA: 213

Peacock, Mr. (attorney): 132

Peck, Quarter Master, USA: 68

Pippin, Dru: 4

Pippin (Tilley), Nancy J.: 5, 193

Pittman, Mary Ann: 187, 188 189

Plummer, Joseph B., BG, USA: 213

Poindexter: 51

Porter, COL, CSA: 64, 75, 214

Post, T. A., LT, USA: 132, 157, 190

Price, Sterling, GEN, CSA: 15-17, 21, 22, 25, 27, 31, 33, 34, 36, 38, 71, 77, 95, 109-113, 185, 203, 213

Pruitt; bushwacker: 109

Pulaski County Democrat: 2, 125

Purcell: 83

Q

Quinn, James, CPT, USA: 118

R

Ray, B.: 66

Ray, J.: 66

Rayl, J. A., PVT, USA: 171, 194, 195

Reavis, J. B., CPT, USA: 53, 55, 56, 58

Reed, Isaac N.: 201

Reeve's Station: 64

Reichert, Francis, LT, USA: 53, 56, 61, 62, 199

Republican Hollow: 128

Reynolds, Thomas C.: 77, 110, 112

Richardson, S. B., CPT, USA: 82, 83, 210

Richardson, Daniel: 66

Riley, Frank; Detective: 179, 185, 186

Roberts, J. R., 2LT, USA: 107

Roland, A.: 66

Rosecrans, William S., GEN, USA: 94, 106, 190

Rotert, Quarter Master, USA: 68

Roubidoux Creek: 2, 5, 41, 51, 80, 118, 128, 142 197, 205

Rydon, W.: 67

S

Sanborn, John B., GEN, USA: 111

Scaggs, William: 66

Schofield Hussars: 77

Schofield, John M., MG, USA: 42, 46, 47, 51, 63, 84, 94, 95, 213

Scott, Winfield, GEN, USA: 34

Shelby, Joseph O. "Jo", GEN, CSA: 15, 45, 49, 84, 85, 87, 114, 186, 188, 189, 213

Shenandoah, CSS: *206*

Sheridan, Philip H., GEN, USA: 35, 36, 202, 218

Sherman, William T., GEN, USA: 15

Shimonoseki, Straits of: 206

Sigel, Albert, MG, USA: 39, 41, 49, 51, 53-56, 58-62, 64, 65, 76, 93, 107, 118, 119, 208, 209

Sigel, Franz, COL, USA: 17, 18, 20, 22, 202, 209, 218

Sinking Creek: 45

Sioux Indians: 202

Slack, GEN, CSA: 213

Smith and Wesson: 118, 209, 210

Smith, A. J., GEN, USA: 113

Smith, Edmond Kirby, GEN, CSA: 78

Smith, Josiah C., CPT, USA: 49, 80-82, 210, 211

Smith, Miss: 109

Smith's Hollow: 200

Snelson, P.: 66

South Carolina, Charleston: 9, 10

Spring Creek Hollow: 109

Stagecoach Stop: 203, 204, 248

Stanley, MG, USA: 213

Stark, Thomas: 67

Steele, Frederick, MG, USA: 63, 64, 75, 213

Stevens, John W. (attorney), LTC, USA: 146, 152, 182

Stith, Mr.: 82

Stone and Son: 67

Storie, Emerson: 50, 207

Storie, Marie: 50, 207

Story, James: 171

Stuart, H. W., Sheriff, CPT: 15

Stuart, William: 66

Sturgis, Samuel D., BG, USA: 21, 213

Sublet, William, PVT, USA: 205

Sweeny, BG, USA: 213

T

Tavern Township: 66, 205

Taylor, Theodore T.: 12

Teeple, Isaac: 66

Teeple, Jacob: 66

Thomas, Thomas, LT, USA: 53, 55, 56, 60

Thompson, CPT, USA: 70

Tillett, CPL, USA: 56, 61

Tilley (Tippett), Elizabeth: 5, 127, 193, 194

Tilley, Bruce "Doc", Dr.: 195

Tilley, Chalotta L.: 5, 193

Tilley, Isaac N.: 5

Tilley, Lee (Vaughn, Jasper L.): 83, 134-187, 195, 193

Tilley, Mahala L. - See Collier, Mahala L.

Tilley, Margaret E. - See Hobbs, Margaret E.

Tilley, Mary Ann - See Morgan, Mary Ann.

Tilley, Missaniah S. - See Bradford, Missaniah S.

Tilley, Nancy J. - See, Pippin, Nancy J.

Tilley, Wilson Leroy: 5, 25, 39, 40, 131-183, 187, 190, 193, 195, 197-199, 202, 210, 211, 213

Tilley, William J.: 5

Tilley, Wilson M.: 4, 5, 7, 8, 23, 67-70, 72, 125-130, 145, 193, 195, 213-215

Tippett, Elizabeth - See Tilley, Elizabeth:

Totton, James, BG, USA: 213

Tucker, S. S. (aka Benson Woods): 80, 211

Turley, James M., MAJ, USA: 121

Turpin, Thomas: 66, 69, 219

Twyford, Charles C., 2LT, USA: 80, 87-91, 133, 143, 211

U

Union Pacific Railroad: 30, 202

V

VanDorn, Earl, GEN, CSA: 36

Vaughan, Maurice: 6

Vaughn, Jasper L.: 5, 173-196

Vaughn, William Franklin: 5

Voelkner, H. A.: 164

W

Waldschmidt, William, LT, USA: 44

Walters, James D., CPT, USA: 53, 56, 59

Warther, Acasden B.: 66

Watie, Stand, GEN, CSA: 130

Watson, Dick: 122

Watson, Thomas H.: 66

Watson, R.: 66

Wayback, Levi L., CPT, USA: 84

Wayman's Mill: 43

Wayman, Mr.: 109

Weaver, Emily: 131, 156, 181, 185-190, 198-200

Westerberg, Napoleon, CPT, USA: 77

Whittle, Lee: 45

Williams, J. H. Dr., USA: 204

Williams, I. S.: 117, 200

Williams, Lewis: 117, 200

Williams, Michael, PVT, USA: 90

Williams: 51

Wilson's Creek, Battle of: 21, 22, 168, 203, 212, 213

Wilson, J. and Son: 67

Wilson, Paymaster, MAJ: 101

Wilson, Roy: 4

Wilson, William: 66, 211

Withers, Charles: 117, 206, 207

Withers, Delilah: 207

Withers, Laura J.: 207

Withers, William D.: 207

Wood, CPT, USA: 29

Woods, Benson (aka Tucker, S. S.): 80, 211

Woods, S. J.: 67

Woods, T.: 67

Woods, W. B., MAJ, USA: 190

Worth, Henry W., CPT, USA: 122

Wright, Clark, LTC, USA: 28, 29, 34

Wright, Thomas, B., LT, USA: 114, 115

Wyoming, USS: *206*

Y

Yahn, T. H., PVT, USA: 100

Japan, country of: 206

York, Judge: 83

Yowell, Widow: 121

Meet The Author

My father was a WWII and Korea Veteran who retired from the U.S. Army after twenty-two years of service. Dad settled our family in Salem, Missouri, and as a result I'm a 1965 graduate of Salem Senior High School. I attended the School of the Ozarks at Pt. Lookout, Missouri and graduated with a bachelor's degree in Sociology in August of 1969. I entered the Missouri State Highway Patrol Academy immediately after college on September 16, 1969. Upon graduation from the MSHP Academy, I was assigned to the Waynesville/Ft. Wood Zone of Troop I in December of 1969. Pulaski County has been my home since then. My career with the Patrol resulted in many commendations, and I'm one of a very small group of Troopers who've been awarded the Medal of Valor by the Missouri State Highway Patrol. I retired as the Local Zone Sergeant in June of 2001. Shortly after retiring, I became a Reserve Officer for the Waynesville City Police.

In 2004, I ran for the elected office of Sheriff of Pulaski County. I won the first race, and I was re-elected for a second four-year term in 2008. The eight years I spent as Sheriff of Pulaski County presented me with more challenges and difficulty than I'd ever faced before. I retired as Sheriff on December 31, 2012. The following week I became a Deputy serving under our new sheriff. I'm currently assigned to the Detective Division as a Reserve Officer who specializes in cases of financial exploitation against older adults. In 2017, I'll start my 47th year in active law enforcement.

I'm married to the former Cheryl Ann Moore of Dixon, Missouri and I have one son, Taylor. I'm a life member of the NRA and a past president of the Old Stagecoach Stop Foundation.

I've written two books about the American Civil War in Missouri. These books are: *The Tilley Treasure*, and *Justice*. The Civil War in Missouri was vastly different from the Civil War that was fought in the southern and eastern states. Both books present the reader with a unique look at how the Civil War affected the border state of Missouri, as citizens struggled to live in a war-torn region. At present, I'm working on several more books based on history and my law enforcement career.

www.ingramcontent.com/pod-product-compliance
Lightning Source LLC
Chambersburg PA
CBHW071212090426
42736CB00014B/2794